Supernature:

how Wilkinson Eyre made a hothouse cool

ORO
EDITIONS

Published by
ORO Editions
Publishers of Architecture, Art, and Design
Gordon Goff: Publisher
www.oroeditions.com
info@oroeditions.com

Copyright © 2013 by ORO Editions
ISBN: 978-1-935935-87-2
10 09 08 07 06 5 4 3 2 1 First edition

Edited by: Emma Keyte
Graphic Design: Margit Millstein
Production Manager: Usana Shadday
Color Separations and Printing: ORO Group Ltd.
Printed in China.

This book was printed and bound using a variety of sustainable manufacturing
processes and materials including soy-based inks, acqueous-based varnish,
VOC- and formaldehyde-free glues, and phthalate-free laminations. The text
is printed using offset sheetfed lithographic printing process in (book specific)
color on 157gsm premium matte art paper with an off-line gloss acqueous
spot varnish applied to all photographs.

ORO Editions makes a continuous effort to minimize the overall carbon
footprint of its publications. As part of this goal, ORO Editions, in association
with Global ReLeaf, arranges to plant trees to replace those used in the
manufacturing of the paper produced for its books. Global ReLeaf is an
international campaign run by American Forests, one of the world's oldest
nonprofit conservation organizations. Global ReLeaf is American Forests'
education and action program that helps individuals, organizations, agencies,
and corporations improve the local and global environment by planting and
caring for trees.

Library of Congress data: Contact for information

For information on our distribution, please visit our website
www.oroeditions.com

Contents

Foreword

Foreword

Nigel Taylor
Director, Singapore Botanic Gardens

Gardens down the ages have represented a strong thread in human culture, their landscapes being measures of our progress as well as being all but essential to our mental well-being. Garden landscapes are also often intimately connected to buildings within them—indeed, in some cases such as sixteenth-century Chinese gardens, the buildings dominate and the gardens' more natural features almost seem to take on the modest role of packaging. Great garden designs—when long-lasting—are challenging to augment with buildings in a way that improves the overall effect. No such challenge applies with new designs that do not have to honour the past. At the Royal Botanic Gardens, Kew (UK) and Gardens by the Bay (Singapore) we have such contrasting situations in equally iconic gardens, one historic, and the other as new as the nation that commissioned it.

Wilkinson Eyre Architects can make a unique claim—that of having designed plant houses that are environmentally cooler than their surroundings in both the temperate and tropical zones. But is this where the similarities end? Undoubtedly not, since the Davies Alpine House at Kew and the Flower Dome and Cloud Forest conservatories at Gardens by the Bay are, by any measure, beautiful structures, but also buildings that need to have high levels of functionality for the health of the living plants they showcase. And both do more than give a casual nod to the now moral obligation for the sustainable use of energy. At Kew, the Davies Alpine House (2006), set within the oldest of British rock gardens, had to compete with its near neighbour, the massive Princess of Wales Conservatory (1987). Similarly it was required to comply with tough specifications from horticultural staff, ever concerned for their specimens' need for abundant light but often less heat than unpredictable British weather delivers. The seamless glass envelope admits all available light, while the nine-metre-tall space within acts as a cooling chimney, drawing cool air from a concrete labyrinth in the foundations to lower the internal daytime temperature—clever! Its striking appearance draws visitors into the Rock Garden, a world of diminutive yet exquisite botanical diversity.

The conservatories within Gardens by the Bay (2012) are on an altogether different scale. As the first time visitor to Singapore arrives in the city from Changi airport they are a cause for wonder, being clearly visible from the East Coast Parkway and making an unmistakeable statement of the vision for a 'City in a Garden' held by this greenest of world cities. The gigantic Flower Dome is breathtaking and the steep-sided Cloud Forest upon entry a jaw-dropping experience, their extravagance tempered by sustainable energy solutions. For the Singaporean these exciting innovations display the plant riches of exotic floras and engender the same wonder the Victorians experienced when Burton & Turner's Palm House opened at Kew in 1848. Here, once again, we see the impact of architect (Wilkinson Eyre), landscaper (Grant Associates), structural engineer (Atelier One), environmental engineer (Atelier Ten) and horticulturist (NParks) coming together in a collaboration that has triumphed in something extraordinary and world class.

above NParks' vision as realised at Gardens by the Bay

Singapore's spring

Dr Tan Wee Kiat
Director, National Parks Board

When we solicited feedback from the public for the proposed development of the Gardens by the Bay in equatorial Singapore, the clamour for comfort and colour in the garden inexorably pointed us in the direction of conservatory construction. The team tasked with turning concept into reality undertook an odyssey to various gardens round the world where notable glasshouses are featured. These conservatories offered controlled tropical, temperate, Mediterranean or alpine conditions, and were invariably developed in gardens north or south of the tropics. We specifically wanted to construct glass envelopes that enclosed environments found in tropical montane cloud forests and in zones featuring a Mediterranean climate, but we wanted these constructions here in Singapore—on a tropical island perched a scant degree north of the equator.

The winning entry by Grant Associates to masterplan the Gardens by the Bay featured two asymmetrical ribbed glass shells impeccably placed along the waterfront of the project site, oriented to allow for an unimpeded trajectory of sunlight from dawn to dusk. Elegantly designed by Paul Baker of Wilkinson Eyre, these two glass shells have to withstand any tremors generated by a neighbouring belt of seismic activity, the onslaughts of monsoon wind and water, and repel sufficient heat from an equatorial sun. The architecture was informed by two years of meticulous research into prototype glasshouses in Singapore conducted by a team led by biologists from the National Parks Board. In a rare alchemy of expertise represented in a team that comprised architect, landscapist, environment and structural engineers in collaboration with the client biologists, the two conservatories were given life as the Flower Dome and the Cloud Forest.

The larger of the two, and covering one hectare, the Flower Dome has two folded 'claws' under its crystal carapace. The bigger claw supports a surreal forest of baobabs and rotund bottle trees amidst caudiciform and pachycaul succulents gathered from four continents. Below this claw, dining space for 800 people beneath a ceiling of programmable lighting bubbles offers not only an extraordinary view of the gardens under glass, but also a magnificent vista of the Singapore waterfront. The smaller claw supports a series of gardens featuring plants from regions that enjoy a Mediterranean climate, including Australia, South Africa, Chile, southern France and California. Four clusters of endemic palms from California, Africa, the Canary Islands and the Andes balance groves of bottle trees from Australia and thousand-year-old olive trees from Spain. Visitors to the Flower Dome arrive at a terrace beneath a fan of metal ribs and glass panels that span free space, subtended by the aforementioned claws, and overlooking a field of flowers that change with the seasons. A moment to recover from the heat and humidity of the tropics, and one is ready for a leisurely stroll down a gentle incline among plants rarely encountered by residents in Singapore's perpetual summer.

In artistic balance to the larger Flower Dome, Wilkinson Eyre designed the smaller but taller Cloud Forest conservatory to house the mini-mountain conceived in response to the vision provided by the client. The 'wow' moment for visitors comes early: the doors swing open to usher visitors to the foot of the tallest indoor waterfall in the world. Cascading some 35 metres in a sheer drop across the face of a plant-covered mountain, the falling waters provide sound to soothe and spray to humidify a cooled environment that supports over 70,000 trees, shrubs and herbs that evoke the lost world of cloud forests around the world.

Less than two months after welcoming the first visitor to Bay South of the Gardens by the Bay, our first millionth visitor arrived, attracted by the twin glass domes of Wilkinson Eyre and the nearby supertrees of Grant Associates. The client team's vision has been realised in full.

left Singapore's Raffles Hotel, c1910

right The Esplanade, Singapore, c1880

below Singapore Botanic Gardens, 1903

A garden for pleasure

Jim Eyre
Director, Wilkinson Eyre Architects

The absolute necessity of plants to our very existence is well known, though disseminating scientific evidence of the psychological benefits for city dwellers of the presence of plants in our immediate environment is relatively new. With more people in the world now living in cities than out of them, Gardens by the Bay seems a timely reminder of the importance of plants to our wellbeing. Many cities are so dense or arid as to lack greenery, at least in the public domain. However, Singapore, though highly populated, has the advantage of being exceptionally verdant. Plants have a special presence, the indigenous jungle has been tamed and Singapore projects itself on the world stage as a 'City in a Garden'—a clever twist on the Garden City concept pioneered in Britain.

Singapore's transformation from its trading origins into a destination city is itself a phenomenon. Once a settlement of genteel houses with verandas, it is now a bustling economic powerhouse of a city with tall buildings, retail emporia, leisure attractions and cultural buildings. The hypermobility of money, goods and people has put cities in an increasingly competitive environment. An ambitious city on the global stage must establish itself as a cultural destination; in this context Singapore cannot exist solely as a port city. Analogous to a garden, its transformation is a work in progress, always evolving, and one could say this transformative work is only now coming into bloom.

Singapore, like Britain, has assimilated diverse influences from other cultures. An example is the legacy left by the British love of gardens and gardening. To the growing influx of Europeans the enveloping jungle spelt danger, so the garden represented an essential cordon sanitaire around the house as well as a resource for play, entertaining and contemplation.

World exploration in the eighteenth and nineteenth centuries gave us the botanic garden system, of which of course, Singapore Botanic Gardens became an important part of the global network, with the hub at Kew in London. Ascendant professional and middle classes had a thirst for knowledge and with it gardening as an activity spread, fuelled by both commercial nurseries and the wonders to be seen in botanic gardens.

Following an earlier, short-lived, garden set up in 1822 by Singapore's founder, Sir Stamford Raffles, it is interesting that the present Botanic Garden was established in 1859 by an agri-horticultural society initially as a leisure garden and ornamental park. Despite this one instance, there is no 'landscape architecture' tradition in Singapore along the lines so well established in Britain by the likes of Humphry Repton, William Kent or Capability Brown. Singapore's climate meant that there was little need to import another product of the industrial age: the system-built conservatory pioneered by Joseph Paxton at Chatsworth and then upscaled to become the world's largest and fastest built structure at the 1851 Great Exhibition in London's Hyde Park.

National Parks' (NParks) ambition for Gardens by the Bay was to create a large scale pleasure garden, distinct from Singapore's botanic garden, which is one of the finest in the world. Botanic gardens emerged in the seventeenth century from the medicinal purpose of physic gardens (the latter dating from the sixteenth-century university gardens in Pisa), not just for the love of science but also for economic reasons. A global network of botanic gardens was established more as essential infrastructure for economic botany exploiting natural resources than as a leisure resource. In this sense visiting botanic gardens could be seen as a fortuitous by-product of their scientific and economic functions.

Pleasure gardens, in contrast, are unmistakably a resource for people and for social interaction. In the west, the concept of the (publicly accessible) pleasure garden originates in eighteenth-century London. Vauxhall Gardens and Ranelagh Gardens were the most famous examples. These were just about the only place where 'respectable' people and the masses could be seen out mixing with one another.

Originally a paying attraction, the pleasure garden allowed the city-dweller to let off steam and get out of the house—and provided something to do on a Sunday. There are plenty of accounts of the form that a visit might take: in the Regency period this varied from an innocent walk to a romantic tryst, through to rather more base encounters and lewd happenings. The pressing need to generate income could be met by providing entertainment within the gardens such as theatres. The example of the Ranelagh Rotunda in London's Chelsea gives an idea of the scale of the operation. The programme would have been quite different from the 'high art' of the West End, a populist offering encouraging more diverse audiences.

In the east, the pleasure garden is a much older idea, with examples thousands of years old of Chinese, Indian and Malay dynasties—and also intellectuals and the governing elite—establishing vast gardens which were no doubt visited by more than emperors and their families. Garden design was a highly developed art form, the intention of classical Chinese gardens in particular being to combine the man-made and the natural in harmonious balance. Many facets of these gardens can be seen—interpreted in contemporary form—at Gardens by the Bay. Water pavilions, for example, are prevalent in Chinese garden architecture, as are artificial mountains or rock forms. The lineage of the conservatories is thereby joined in its ancestry by roots from both east and west.

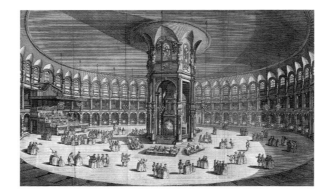

top Woodcut from the *Illustrated London News* showing the ascent of the Nassau Balloon from Vauxhall Gardens in 1836

middle Interior of the Ranelagh Rotunda

bottom Early nineteenth-century view of a Chinese Mandarin's palace, with garden, pool and water pavilions

left Wilkinson Eyre's 2003 site development plan for the Royal Botanic Gardens, Kew, proposing a new arc of buildings, installations and planted features to draw visitors out into the landscape

right The Davies Alpine House seen in context

The evocatively named Cloud Mountain and Flower Dome conservatories at Gardens by the Bay are part of a project that turns many of our expectations and traditions on their head, holding up our fragile environment as if to a mirror, with ourselves in the foreground cast in a new light. Even the land on which they rest wasn't always land at all, but was reclaimed from the sea. The Mediterranean climate reproduced in Flower Dome houses plants from one of the most marginal environments endangered by climate change. Likewise the Cloud Mountain displays the narrow band of temperate rainforest or montane habitat. The environment within the conservatories is the opposite of what one expects of a glasshouse—the hothouse of our book's title is cooled to be a lower temperature than outside. In Britain we would be worried about condensation forming on the inside due to the warmth and humidity meeting the thin barrier of glass separating it from our cold climate; in Singapore it's the other way round and the enclosure must be double-glazed. In eighteenth-century London, nature was used as a setting for unrelated entertainment, but here nature itself becomes theatre. The idea of the pleasure garden as a relief for the inhabitants of the city develops into a cultural landmark that brings people to the city. This city that owes its existence to trade and transit of goods is transforming itself as a global destination for people.

The pleasure gardens of London died partly because of their disreputable activities within, but also because of the advent of the railways and the ease with which city dwellers could reach the seaside. In Singapore transportation brings people in the opposite direction and, in a state where good behaviour is the norm, what is more innocent than a visit to the public gardens?

Plants and people are phototropic: we are drawn towards the available light. And similarly Wilkinson Eyre was drawn irresistibly to this project. Our interest in gardens and landscape was stimulated by work we undertook at Kew for the then-director Sir Peter Crane, generating a site development plan to support their successful application to become a UNESCO World Heritage Site. Emerging from that masterplan was our design for the Davies Alpine House—an innovative low-energy glasshouse for keeping plants dry and cool. As architects we have always been motivated by a desire to make structures work hard and be as elegant as possible, bringing out the qualities we admire of lightness and slenderness. Coupled with our experience in designing visitor attractions and even acting as exhibition designers, the Gardens by the Bay conservatories represented the ideal project.

An architectural critique

Edwin Heathcote

As more and more cities attempt the difficult transition to world-city status, each is having to work harder to define itself, to find within it something which distinguishes itself from all the other metropolises bustling and jockeying for position. And the harder they try, the more they tend to look the same. Those busy skylines crammed with glassy towers, the mega-malls populated by the ubiquitous luxury brands, the chain hotels and the pedestrianised shopping streets and the waterfront walks with chilled al fresco seating. These are settings often constructed from seemingly nothing, from an unlikely desert, reclaimed land or the once bleak landscape of a post-industrial dockside. Singapore is a place that lacks the topographical drama of Hong Kong or the industrial solidity of Bilbao. Its equatorial weather is stickily humid and its new swathes of land are being clawed back at great expense from beneath the sea. But Singapore's solution to distinctiveness has been striking—it is the effort to use its particular climatic conditions to make itself a city of green. This idea has been officially termed by the government the transformation to a 'City in a Garden'. From the bougainvillea-lined roads to the planters and trees which punctuate its streets, Singapore's plan has been sprouting in the way in which only a place with this level of control and central planning can.

And at the very heart of that plan is Gardens by the Bay. An extraordinary effort which aims to emulate the success of Manhattan's Central Park or central London's Royal Parks by creating a 54-hectare green heart, a landscape from nothing, reclaimed from the sea and hugely extending the island's stock of city centre prime property in the process.

The context is odd, perhaps even a little overwhelming. The adjacent Marina Bay Sands complex is a monster, a strange, sci-fi echo of a futuristic Stonehenge, a 55-storey complex topped by a 'skypark' looming in the background. There is no competing with it. Moshe Safdie's huge 'Integrated Resort' (Singapore is still, despite the scale of a complex which out-earns Las Vegas, a little squeamish about the word 'casino') stamps its authority on the newly reclaimed land but also stomps out any possible competition. How can a park possibly compete with an architectural object on that scale? How can the new gardens assert themselves on the skyline? The flat reclaimed land offered few possibilities for the kind of dramatic landscaping that would have allowed the gardens to become a feature able to compete with the city's burgeoning architectural profile. So this would need to be an eccentric kind of landscape, a garden with a verticality to echo Singapore's spiky skyline and an intervention with a theatricality to be able to create a place from seemingly nothing.

Perhaps gardens in the centre of Singapore were never going to be serene. In fact, just as nature itself goes into a kind of tropical overdrive in the permanent summer of an equatorial climate, so the gardens accommodate a kind of hypernature, a pumped up vision of nature as theatre.

The result is the pair of vast glass conservatories which embed the gardens in the cityscape alongside the vertical mushrooming of the supertrees, the complex webs of futuristic armature which create green-clad skyscrapers within the gardens.

top Conservatories and supertrees at the Bay South garden

bottom Moshe Safdie's Marina Bay Sands resort towers over the Gardens by the Bay site

left An aerial view of the gardens reveals the Marina Barrage and development zone beyond

The cocktail of architecture, engineering and turbo-charged nature presents an extraordinary vision, something surprising, surreal and, on occasion, truly breathtaking. It is strikingly original in its strangeness yet it also creates a landscape which builds on familiar precedents. At the Royal Botanic Gardens Kew, Sir William Chambers' Japanese pagoda is as much a part of the landscape as Decimus Burton's Palm House. These were garden follies brought into the industrial age, their scale hypertrophying to match the striking bridges, mills, factory chimneys and railway stations which had turned Britain's cities into a new type of place. Nicholas Grimshaw recognised that the post-industrial age demanded a grand gesture of its own to create a place of the abandoned quarry of the Eden Project and Wilkinson Eyre's work at Gardens by the Bay recognises that same need to scale up to the context.

This is a garden that needs to compete with the waterfront skyscraper lightshows of Hong Kong and the endless artificial islands of the Gulf. It needs to hold its own against theme parks and casinos, against self-consciously iconic museums and opera houses, it is landscape inflated to architecture to create a distinctive profile for an island that has lagged behind in the building of logo architecture. But, unlike most of those attractions, the gardens at Bay South are also real public space. Just as Frederick Law Olmsted created Central Park as a lung for a dense city, this landscape is intended to open up the heart of Singapore.

It is not pure municipal philanthropy. A convenient and calculated side effect of amenity of the gardens is value. The Bay South garden is also a canny move to create desirability to developers in the proposed grid of streets that will surround it. In a move of financial magic it begins to pay for itself as surrounding land, owned by the government (which has historically kept a tight control on housing) leaps in value. This is truly a novel approach. The cities of the Gulf may have attempted land reclaims of equal or greater ambition with the Worlds and the Pearls and the endless Palms but these were always primarily about the creation of luxury enclaves. Their failure, or at least their stagnation, has illustrated the dangers of undertaking such vast schemes as private ventures. Singapore's approach has been different. Here the gardens have been created as a civic space at the heart of what it is hoped will be a series of new urban districts—but it is not dependent on them. The plans for the future are ambitious but achievable. The expansion of the mass transit system to create a new connection will in turn create the impetus for a flower market at the entrance to the gardens. This, it is hoped, will create a vibrant commercial buzz as well as a de facto souvenir shop bridging the gardens, the city and its infrastructure. The spectacle here is at the service of the city rather than of private wealth.

The Gardens are asked to do many things; they drag landscape into the realm of architecture and create from a place of artifice a simulated natural landmark. They expand the city centre across the bay and they create a huge new green public realm in a densely populated city. And they do it with a verve that takes the breath away.

Wilkinson Eyre's two huge biomes appear almost like a great humpbacked creature emerging from the sea. In fact, from the beginning, the architects adopted the idea that these twin structures would appear in the landscape like giant invaders, alien objects which thrived off the landscape but which also fed back into it through their presence. The two great glasshouses are similar structures, one flatter and broader, the other taller and sharper, as if it were a squeezed version of the other. Each is conceived as an array of structural steel arcs braced by a gridshell.

The larger of the two has been dubbed the Flower Dome. Covering 1.2 hectares and rising to 38 metres high, the structure contains the cool, dry climate of the Mediterranean and its purpose is to house the kind of colourful flowers and plants that would otherwise not thrive in Singapore's climate. It was launched in an explosion of colour with the astonishing World Orchid Conference of 2011.

right Interior of the Flower Dome during the World Orchid Conference 2011

below The conservatories, as seen from Marina Bay

left Interior of the Cloud Forest

above left The conservatories' two structural systems – steel ribs and gridshell

above right The structural systems as read from inside

The other glasshouse has become known as the Cloud Forest. With an artificial mountain at its core, this structure (covering 0.8 hectares and rising to 58 metres high) replicates the cool, moist conditions of a tropical mountainside. A 35-metre waterfall gushes to permeate the structure with sound and a welcome spray of fine mist, conditions which also create strange low-level clouds that hug the ground at certain times of day.

The discrete nature of the ribcage and gridshell structures of the conservatories allows the two structural systems to be read separately. From the outside the glass appears to be floating within a cage of curving arches, from the inside the glass shell is read as a complete system casting a shadowed grid on the ground. The way the two systems barely seem to touch reinforces an idea of weightlessness whilst the contiguous nature of the roof, its supports not entirely visible from within, evokes that idea of the endless interior that was once the ultimate fantasy of modernism, a lineage that embraces Bruno Taut's Crystal Cathedrals as much as it does Buckminster Fuller's geodesic domes and his drawing of a Manhattan sheltered under a massive glass roof.

But it also refers to a kind of perennial modern condition; the airport, the megamall and the oversized atrium, the theme park and the holiday resort. Just as the great glasshouses of the nineteenth century could not avoid being compared to the railway station roofs and the exhibition halls of Victorian Britain, neither can these conservatories escape the comparison to the ubiquitous spaces of continuous interior modernity. But whilst the Victorian glasshouses, the Crystal Palace and the London rail termini contained the fruits and the tools of the industrial revolution, these biomes protect a simulacrum of nature. The reversal of that century and a half is striking. In the Victorian era these complex and delicately beautiful structures were used to give status and testament to the products of industry and artifice, now their twenty-first-century equivalents contain natural, organic worlds.

That story of nature has become a defining narrative of the modern age. As cities strip us further from any reminders of an agricultural or rural history, so nature takes on a kind of magic aura. The notion of sustainability becomes a mantra, a semi-religious incantation. It also raises some difficult questions for a project like this. There can be no realistic pretence that this is a sustainable architecture and Singapore's own credentials as a sustainable city have been questioned—its carbon emissions per capita are among the highest in Asia and indeed the world. It is obviously folly to attempt to claim green credentials for a recreation of a cool climate in the midst of a steamy equatorial fug. It is, in fact, difficult for a northern-European mind to accept at all the idea of creating a greenhouse in a tropical climate, a greenhouse for keeping things cool.

Yet having said that, the biomes do what they can, and often in intriguing ways. The design acknowledges that hot air rises. These are not completely cooled interiors. Instead the cooling is confined to where the plants and people are, directed and aimed at the slivers of populated space. Where conditions turn more tropical, for instance in the upper levels of the Flower Dome, the terraces are populated by baobab trees which appreciate the sweaty conditions. Then there is the shading, the harlequin pattern of the sunshades, which unfurl across the roofs and radically change the nature of the glass roofs from carapace to canopy. The other argument for sustainability is based on education. Gardens by the Bay is pure edutainment, aimed at a mass market for whom gardening has not been a significant hobby. To pull people in, the designers have had to aim at the spectacular but once they are in visitors might find themselves learning as a side effect. Low lying tropical Singapore is likely to be one of the places to suffer earliest and most severely from climate change and a rise in sea levels. A critical part of the Gardens' mission is to inculcate this sense of nature as a beautiful spectacle but a not always entirely benign force.

left Terraced planting in the Flower Dome

right The Flower Dome with sunshades unfurled

At the centre of the vision are the two huge biomes. Their forms were initially inspired by an early conceptual drawing of a garden planned around the shape of an orchid, with the biomes as the flowering head. These are huge spaces—among the biggest greenhouses in the world—and the scale, so far beyond the normal proportions of buildings, helps them to fade away. The continuous nature of the gridshell, the lack of walls and discrete roofs, the lack of vertical, orthogonal surfaces allows the focus to fall on the plants and the skywalks that thread through the landscapes.

The supertrees, designed by Grant Associates, are a different matter. These are self-conscious sculptural markers to allow the park to compete with the city's towers. Their shape sits somewhere between mushrooms and cocktail parasols, or perhaps exotic flowers and Perpendicular vaulting. Some of these supertrees act as chimneys for the exhaust air created to power the biomes, some support arrays of solar panels in their crowns but the largest of them becomes a building in its own right, its interior inserted by Wilkinson Eyre, a spectacular viewing tower. The armatures of the supertrees, complex welded webs of steel rods, are designed not only as striking, sci-fi structures but to encourage the growth of epiphytes so

that the gardens' greenery sends its tendrils upwards towards the sky. At night they become beacons to equal Hong Kong's skyline lightshow, a throbbing *son-et-lumière* extravaganza which lights up the city, an obligatory tourist photo stop. The lightshow allows the gardens to become part of the city's vision of itself in a way that greenery on its own could never do. Its quirky attitude to sustainability is expressed precisely in drawing attention to nature through scale and drama, through verticality and exponential growth as well as to an architecture that is its adjunct and its servant whilst still exerting an impact itself. But it is also sustainable in that it creates a vibrant public place for the city. The biomes may be ticketed but the gardens are open and accessible, a place to stroll and appreciate the city in the pleasant evening air. Just as the water in the bay around it has been cut off from the sea so that it will slowly become a fresh water lagoon supplying an ever thirstier city, so the gardens will begin to catalyse the centre of the city into a more open, greener place where reference and adjacency to nature is possible in a way it is often not elsewhere.

above Night view of the gardens across Marina Bay

This is an extraordinary landscape, a garden for a sci-fi city that recalls some of the most ambitious filmic tropes of utopian production design. It is nature hyped up, encouraged upwards and to grow exponentially, an Atlantis in reverse, a landscape drawn back up from beneath the sea. Its strangeness and its theatricality enable it to give greenery the prominence to allow it to compete with architecture and urbanism. It is an intriguing urban experiment which places the park at the heart of the new city and attempts to use the artifice of managed nature not to relieve the monotony of the city but to generate a new urban quarter based around a generous civic and public realm of enhanced green.

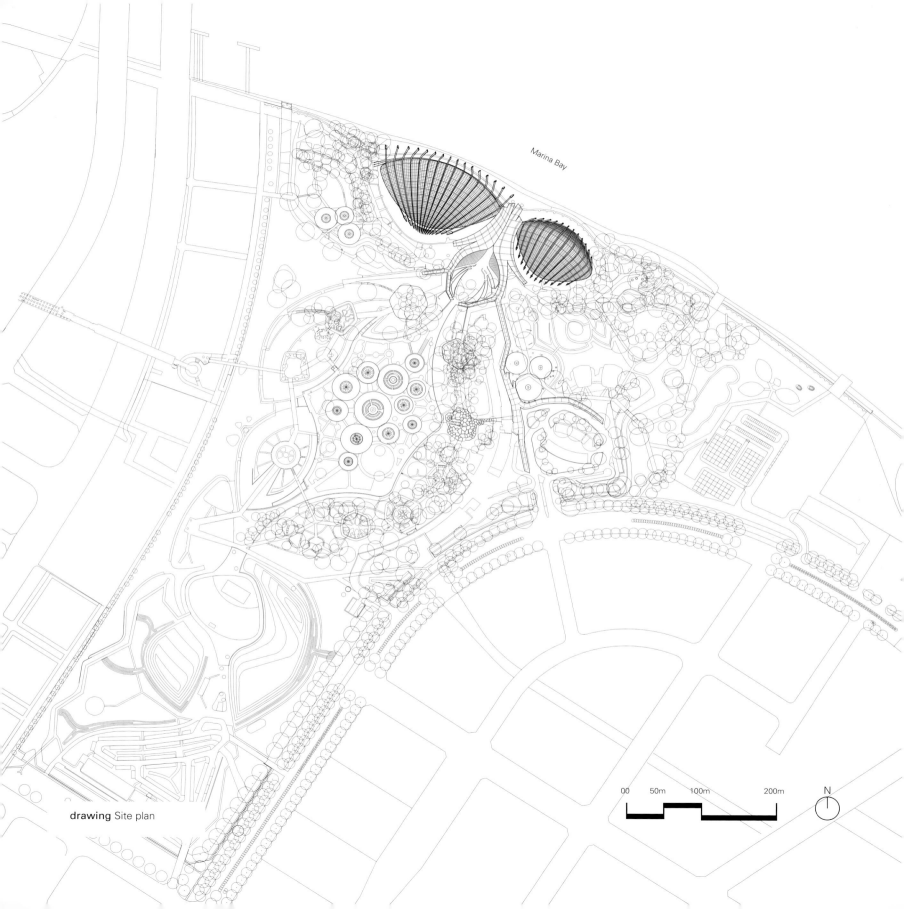

Marina Bay

drawing Site plan

00　50m　100m　　　　200m

N

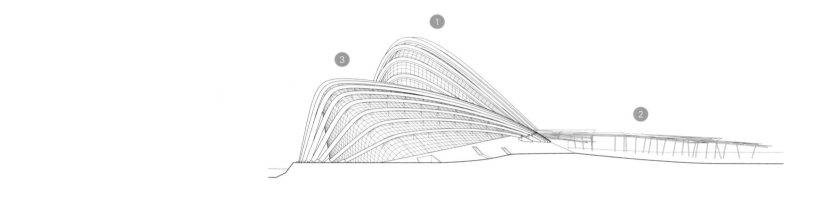

1 Cloud Forest
2 Hub / Canopy
3 Flower Dome

drawings West elevation (top); north elevation (bottom)

00 10m 20m   40m

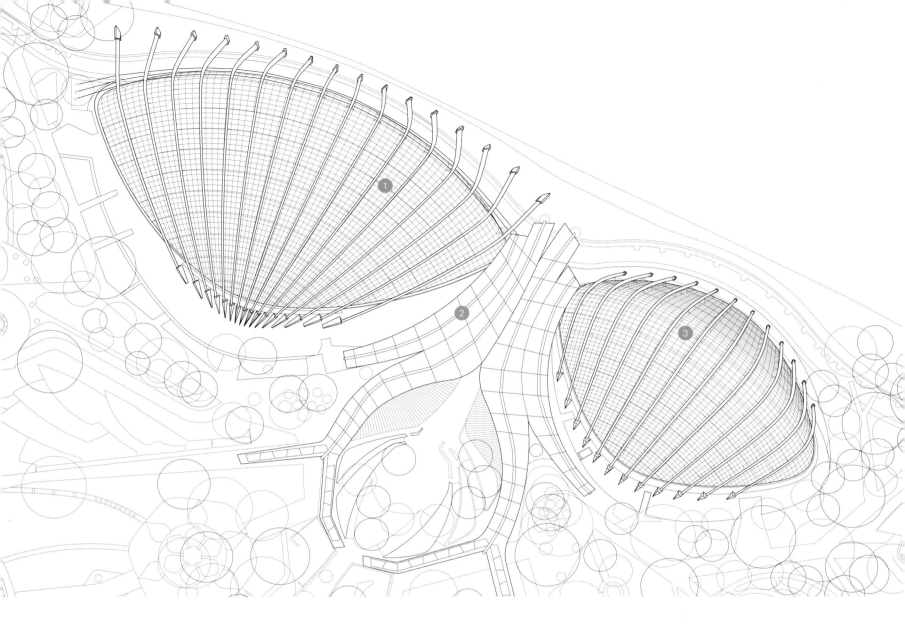

1 Flower Dome
2 Hub / Canopy
3 Cloud Forest

drawing Roof plan

00   15m   30m   60m   N

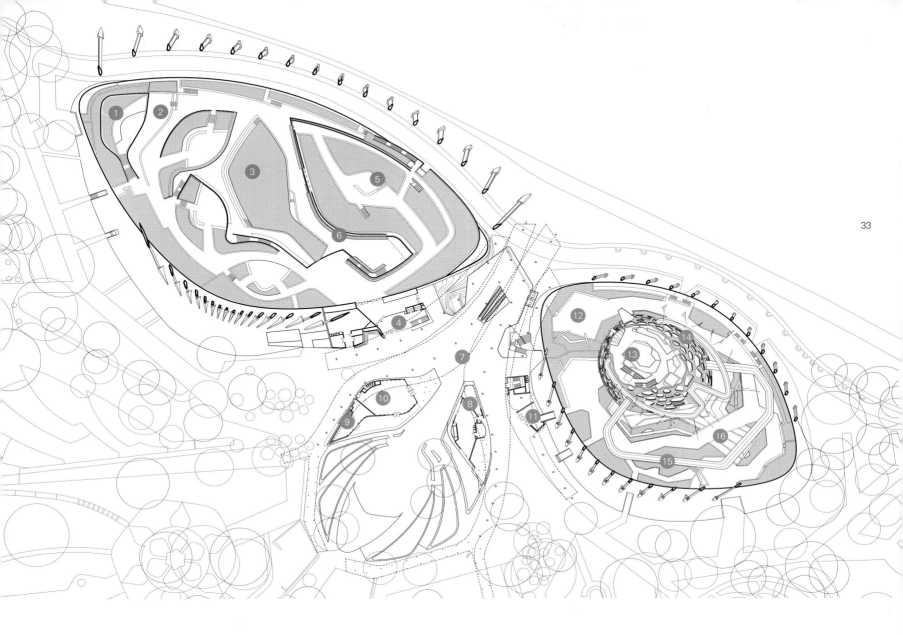

1 Pollen restaurant (below)
2 Olive Grove
3 Flower Field
4 Flower Dome group entry
5 Baobabs
6 Event space (below)
7 Hub / Canopy
8 Ticketing

9 Canopy café
10 Retail
11 Cloud Forest group entry
12 Forest Walk
13 Lost World
14 Cloud Walk
15 Treetop Walk
16 Ravine

00   15m   30m   60m   N

drawing Ground plan

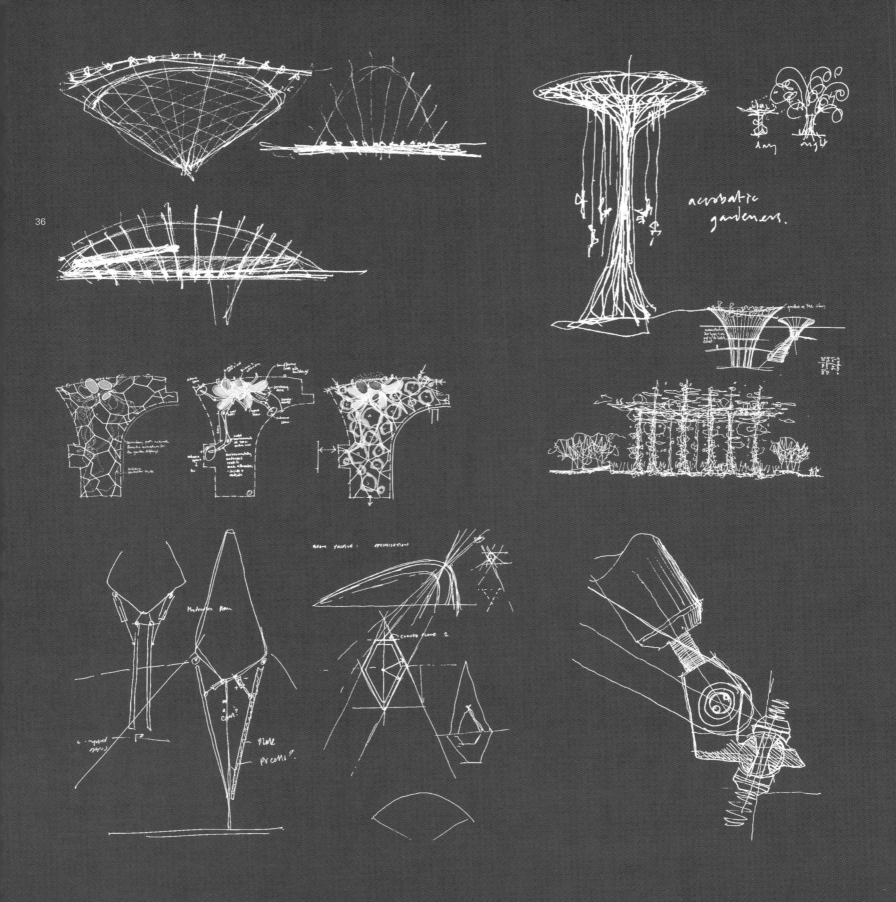

36

acrobatic gardeners.

Sketching

Paul Baker
Director, Wilkinson Eyre Architects

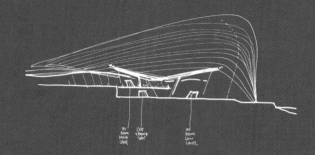

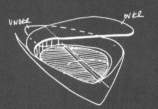

Sketching lay at the heart of the design process for Gardens by the Bay. I truly believe that a good sketch can speak a thousand words and on this project, with its multinational, multilingual team, drawing became the language through which we communicated many of our best and most complex thoughts. Talking in sketches, sketching on each others' sketches, is a sign of a well-functioning team properly investigating design ideas together. Sometimes the sketches are beautiful and sometimes they are extremely rough, but it doesn't matter as long as they convey the essence of the idea.

Andrew Grant—an unstoppable sketcher—would often arrive for meetings at our London office armed with piles of beautiful, brightly coloured sketches he had drawn on the train up from Bath. Whenever we were met with a particularly difficult technical issue to do with the structural design, Neil Thomas would fax us an exploratory sketch which our team could then explore further in CAD. These sketches were pivotal in helping us understand how the whole thing would work. Patrick Bellew's team in turn produced clever, explanatory drawings and flowcharts showing how the different elements of the masterplan could be connected to create an ecosystem across the site.

For us, the architectural team, countless sketches of the conservatory forms helped us to refine the aesthetic and explore how the arrangement of the structural ribs could enhance their organic shape. These rough-and-ready conceptual sketches developed into more considered ones, sometimes using the 3D model as a background. Later in the process, our site-based team would often hand-draw on site visits, sketching over the construction drawings to explain finer points of the design to the contractors.

The selection of sketches shown here give a flavour of this drawn language, which was ultimately so important in the collaborative process.

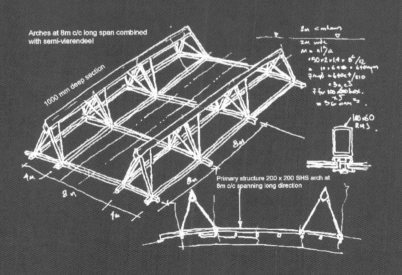

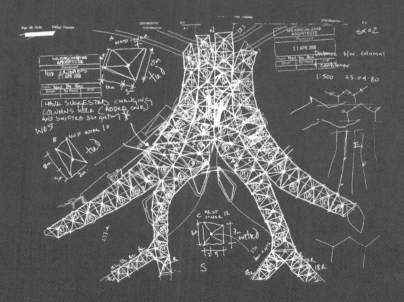

CAD modelling

Many people have commented, on seeing photographs of Gardens by the Bay, that the structures look 'just like CGIs'. The comment is apt; these are buildings which we could not have created without computer-generated images. Alongside sketching, CAD modelling was one of the primary tools for the design team, helping us to sculpt, test, build, describe and promote the buildings.

Squint Opera's film, made as part of the competition bid and shown in the screengrabs below, describes the methodology adopted by the team during the early stages of the project. It was an iterative process, with pin-up boards covered in snippets from the brief, ideas and reference images, and sketches of all kinds—both hand- and computer-drawn. For many members of the team—particularly the younger generation—designing on screen with keyboard and mouse is as fast and intuitive as hand sketching, and so the CAD sketches became as prolific as the pencil ones.

We used these sketches, rapidly created in Rhino, to visualise the three-dimensional spaces within the conservatories—and outside of them. They allowed us to experiment with beautiful forms and then accurately measure their dimensions, carry out preliminary assessments of how the environmental systems might work, and massage them to meet the requirements of the brief. The work in CAD acted as a counterpoint to our hand-sketching, although the two techniques were also used simultaneously, with new ideas often drawn on trace over printouts of the Rhino models.

The CAD work was often used as the basis for other design activity—so, for example, they were given to the modelmaking team for translation into physical models, and to Grant Associates, who added layers of planting in Photoshop to indicate the look and feel of the spaces when built. Even the interiors in the Squint Opera film are built on these same models. Later in the process, the CAD models provided a means to explore technical ideas—for example, studying the interfaces between cladding and structure, or resolving the geometry of the shading systems. We used snapshots from these models to swiftly relate technical ideas to the rest of the design and construction team, so they still needed to look appealing.

There was real craft in much of this work: it was as much about representation as it was about construction and calculation. There was a desire to create CAD images which had a certain elegance, which would convey a sense of space without necessarily being photorealistic.

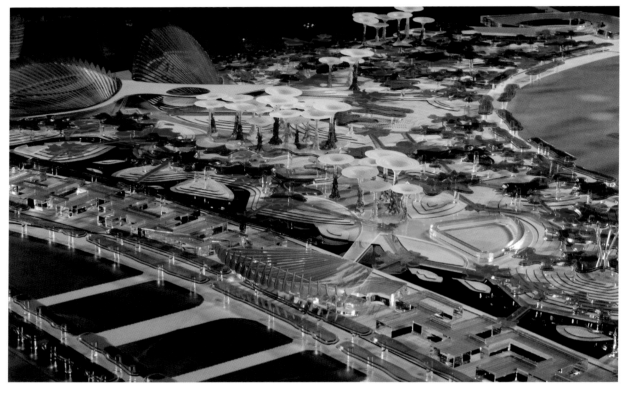

 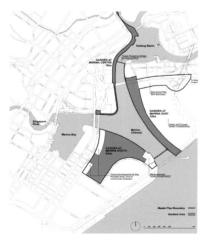  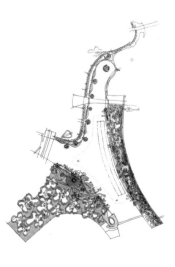

top Networks Modelmakers' perspex competition model illustrated our design vision for all three Gardens by the Bay sites

bottom left to right Diagrams from the competition brief showing the location of the three gardens in relation to future development and massing, refined in Andrew Grant's concept sketch (far right)

Competition

above Shots from an early site visit show views across the bay and existing avenues of trees

In early 2006, Wilkinson Eyre was approached by Grant Associates to join a team they were fielding for an exciting new design competition in Singapore. The practices had worked together on a number of projects and competitions—a major commercial development in central London, large cultural buildings and a series of schools in southern England—but this represented a much closer collaboration and a far more ambitious scheme. The brief immediately captured the imagination: a vast garden on an already spectacular waterfront, and at its heart a tricky technical challenge to create cool conservatory environments quite alien to Singapore's tropical climate. It was an irresistible opportunity to further expand our geographical and design horizons.

The client, NParks, had a strong vision for the new Gardens by the Bay, not just in terms of their horticultural programme, but also in reinforcing the city's social and environmental offer. The idea was that the project would epitomise Singapore's transformation into a 'City in a Garden', "in which pervasive greenery is linked and integrated with the urban fabric, creating an intense and seamless experience that extends from streetscape to sky gardens". Three waterfront gardens—each with a distinct personality and planted content—would form part of a huge, 11-kilometre waterfront promenade linking a range of public attractions. Built on recently reclaimed land (the newest sections were only reclaimed during the 1990s), they would attract locals and visitors to the bay, which in turn would become a focus for celebration and recreational activities.

Our team, led by Grant Associates, was announced as joint winner (with Gustafson Porter) of the design competition in autumn 2006. Although the original competition had required concept designs for all three gardens, it was decided that the gardens at Bay East and Bay Central would be given to Gustafson Porter and local teams for development over the longer term, while the Grant Associates team would immediately progress the largest of the gardens at Bay South.

The 54-hectare site is the largest public open space on Marina Bay, and sits within a district of rapid commercial, leisure and residential development. This location puts it at centre stage in the emerging composition of destination buildings around the waterfront. The focal point of the site—and the anchor attraction within the gardens—is the cooled conservatory complex, for which Wilkinson Eyre took the design lead. Simultaneously an architectural icon, horticultural attraction and showcase of sustainable technology, the complex showcases plants from the areas of the world most vulnerable to climate change—the Mediterranean and tropical montane climate zones. Covering an area in excess of 20,000 square metres, the conservatories are among the largest climate-controlled glasshouses in the world.

Masterplan

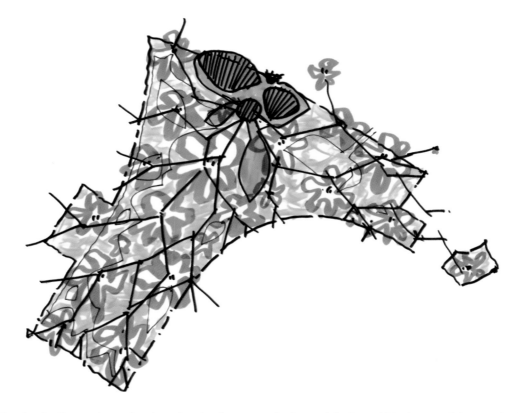

left Site masterplan for Bay South

above Andrew Grant's early concept sketch for the masterplan, inspired by the stems of an orchid, Singapore's natural flower

The masterplan for the gardens, developed under the leadership of Grant Associates, reinforces a series of narrative themes. The orchid is the national flower of Singapore, and closely informed our early concept designs for the conservatories. The bifurcated stems of the orchid are represented by circulation routes across the site connecting the conservatories with the various individual outdoor gardens and clusters of supertrees— vertical gardens up to 50 metres in height. These routes also link to key points of entry into the site, helping to knit the garden into the surrounding urban fabric.

Just as epiphytic orchids draw moisture and nutrients from their surrounding environment, the conservatories are akin to positively beneficial symbiotic organisms, the gardens sustaining them and vice versa through an integrated environmental system which is also linked to the supertrees. Within this context, the conservatories contain a collected landscape, acting as giant cloches that cover sections of this landscape and transform it through their specific climatic characteristics, allowing foreign plants from other environmental zones to grow and flourish.

44 Locating the conservatories was integral to the masterplanning process. Some of the other competition entries had placed the conservatories deep into the gardens; others had positioned them apart or even as integrated structures under a single roof. However, with the districts around the site intended for dense high-rise development, we felt that overshadowing on the site would become a critical factor. The waterfront was the only place on the site that was always going to get good light. But locating the conservatories here was also about creating a relationship between gardens and bay. We were conscious that the conservatories' presence on the waterfront would give them maximum public exposure, allowing them to become part of Singapore's visual identity. They were envisaged as organic landforms which would add a new element to the composition of landmarks around the bay, part of the picture postcard view of the city and highly visible on the approach from the airport.

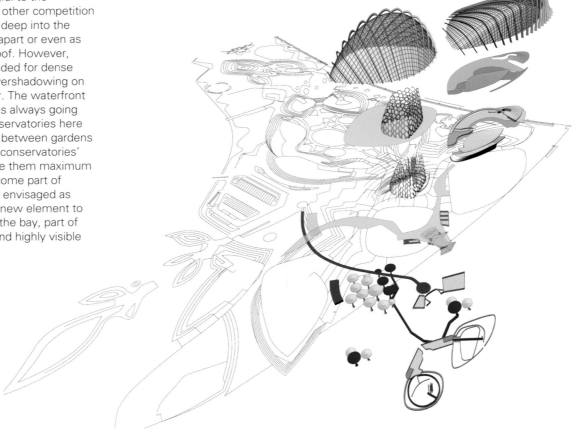

From first principles

Neil Thomas
Director, Atelier One

45

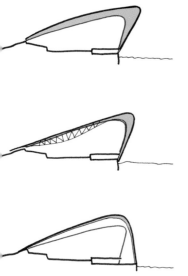

left top Exploded axonometric showing the interlinked built elements of the masterplan

left bottom The conservatories viewed as landforms from across the bay

below Sketches exploring structural strategies for achieving the Flower Dome's tilt

below right Sectional sketches showing evolution of gridshell and glazing profile to maximise daylight and minimise shadows

The structural brief for the cooled conservatories was driven by the statement "the plants are your client"—we needed to allow as much light into the conservatories as was possible to achieve maximum plant growth. The structure was developed in conjunction with Wilkinson Eyre, and in its final form combines two different structural systems—a gridshell and stiffened arches. The whole collaborative process by which we reached this solution can be illustrated in just one diagram, seen below, which shows how we developed the profile for the gridshell. Although simple, it represents years of work in how we came to understand the extremely clever stratified temperature principle within the conservatory, combined with the potential thermal movement of a huge steel structure.

The gridshell draws from the basic structural principle known as geometric (shape) stiffness and is borrowed from seashells—abundant in nature—in which the form carries the load. For us, this seemed the obvious structural solution for the forms we were trying to create, with their double curvature and large spans. By reducing the 'shell' of the conservatories to a light structural mesh or grid, obstruction to sunlight is reduced as very little structure is actually required. By then evolving the profile of the structural members, it was possible to introduce even more daylight into the building.

Shells, however, are very sensitive. The Flower Dome gridshell at Gardens by the Bay is 170 metres across and the very thin surface, although capable of carrying its own self-weight, would buckle in high winds. Once again, nature provided a solution. Large shells often have stiffening ribs and so these were added in the form of arches, which were eventually pulled away from the gridshell surface to reduce the light silhouette. Furthermore, the diagram shows how the enclosure profile developed, with the glazed skin evolving from being first suspended to finally sitting outside the shell structure.

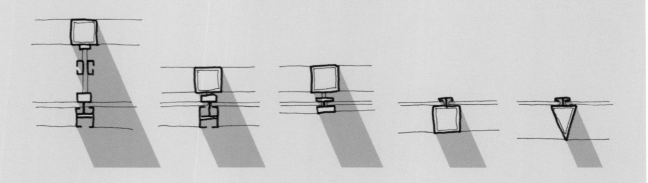

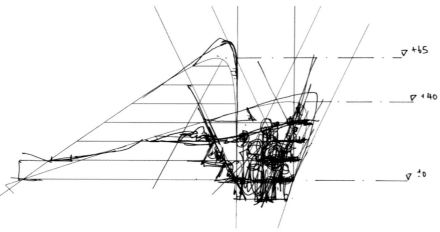

above The complementary forms of the conservatories, viewed from Marina East: *"When you look at the two of them together, it's a complete experience, both emotionally and spatially."* Paul Baker

left Early sketch showing the development of these forms

Developing the design

From the start, our strategy was to place the two required growing environments—Mediterranean and tropical montane—in separate structures. The brief did not require this, but we felt that it made sense to have two different environments that formed a family through their complementary content, narrative and forms. However, we worked hard to develop a distinct personality for each in terms of their geometric expression, in response to the contrasting environments within.

In an age where CAD and CAM are evolving fast, buildings whose complex forms are computer generated have almost become the norm. We have always enjoyed the liberating effects that advancing technologies have enabled, giving us the ability to work with curvilinear forms to exploit their inherent potential for visual dynamism. However, our interest in geometry is governed by a belief that an underlying rationale to curved geometrical forms is critical in establishing a sense of architectural order—as well as helping us to achieve the elegance that Wilkinson Eyre always aims for. We like to experiment with geometry with a degree of rigour, either using known geometries to find preconceived forms or else the reverse—developing new forms from a rational geometry. The other benefit of this discipline in how we deploy geometry—and in the constant refinement of the forms that are created—is that we are able to achieve a sense of lightness, of legibility and even a sense of arrested movement.

And so it is perhaps no surprise that in Singapore, although we originally experimented with a range of forms for the structures, we inevitably returned to first principles and proven geometries. Though buildings traditionally make use of right-angled forms (for good reason), nature does not. As a project concerning the fundamental aspects of nature, Gardens by the Bay presented a clear case for deriving a form that responded to environmental and contextual cues rather than conventional orthogonal geometries.

Our desire was to make elegant forms that would complement the concepts emerging in parallel for the wider garden. However, the primary inputs into establishing the particular forms of the conservatories were complex: we needed to maximise the incidence of daylight penetrating the structure; we had to achieve the required footprint (the Flower Dome has 10,100 square metres under glass and the Cloud Forest 6,300 square metres), ideally with a clear span; we wanted to achieve a strong sense of the sky above and soaring interior spaces, not just for the experience but also to achieve temperature stratification; and we needed to respond to the proximity of the waterfront, running along the northern edge of the site. Added to this was the apparently irreconcilable challenge of making cooled conservatories in a hot, humid climate in the most sustainable way possible. With this in mind, it was clear to us that a curved enclosure would be the most efficient way—in terms of both cost and potential heat gain—of enclosing as much volume as possible with the smallest amount of envelope, and therefore an organic, curvilinear form became the focus of our design attention.

48

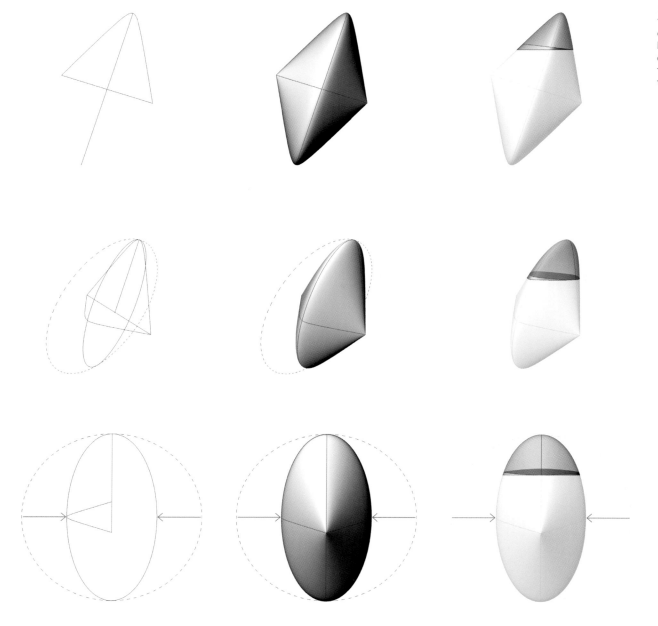

left Diagrams showing
the generation of the
conservatory geometry
by rotating a hyperbolic
curve and taking a cut
through the resultant
three-dimensional form

49

bottom left By tipping the toroidal shape, the Flower Dome is made to gesture towards the bay

bottom right The related geometries of the Cloud Forest and Flower Dome

We naturally looked back at what we had done before, as many of the buildings and bridges Wilkinson Eyre have designed have drawn from geometric and organic forms. We were looking for a pure geometry from which we could derive the two complementary forms and then spend time manipulating them to make them more definable and easy to build. Inevitably we were influenced by the experience we had had in designing the Davies Alpine House at Kew (also a cooled conservatory), which was composed from two pairs of parabolic arches. These arches created the height necessary to draw warm air out of the building (via a stack effect) within a relatively small footprint, and so we began experimenting with a similar parabolic form.

The forms that emerged were generated by rotating a hyperbolic curve around an axis to create a toroidal form, and then taking a slanting cut through it to create the ground plane of the buildings. We then undertook many studies to manipulate these forms, in particular taking into account the orientation and composition of the buildings on the waterfront. In the case of the larger Flower Dome, the entire shape was tipped over so its waterfront façade is inclined inwards. This corresponds to the maximum northerly track of the 'winter' sun to avoid the need for additional shading on this northern façade, and allowing views out across the bay to be maintained. The Cloud Forest started with a similar geometry but we found that we needed to compress or scale the form along its axis to create a smaller footprint in relation to the greater height that we sought in order to contain the mountain within.

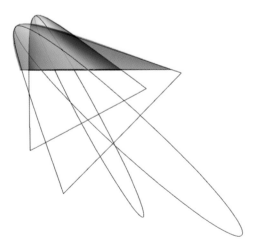

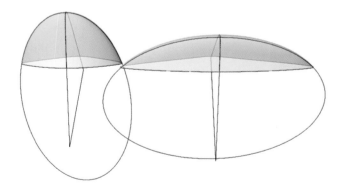

Both biomes have a composite structure comprising a gridshell that works in tandem with a superstructure of radially arranged steel ribs. The structural design was informed by the briefing requirement that as much daylight as possible should enter the buildings to create the appropriate growing environments—and also our aforementioned desire to achieve a clear span, unobstructed by the presence of significant internal supporting trusses. A steel gridshell—a structure constructed from a grid lattice which derives strength from its curvature—appeared to be the most appropriate solution, at least initially. However, we were worried that a pure gridshell would not be strong enough to cope with the uneven loads that would be placed on it in high winds. Stiffening the gridshell to make it stronger would have made the structure too heavy and cut out too much of the daylight, particularly on the Flower Dome, so the ribs were introduced to stabilise it. These ribs not only address the lateral loads to the gridshell but also provide the conservatories with their distinctive organic appearance.

The ribs, which are linked by steel struts to the gridshell below, were subject to an in-depth geometric study to establish a cross-sectional form that would emphasise their lightness as well as minimise obstruction to daylight. This section tapers along the length of each rib in relation to the loads placed upon it. As they meet the ground, the ribs are based in concrete shoes and are painted off-white to reflect light and heat and reduce their thermal expansion.

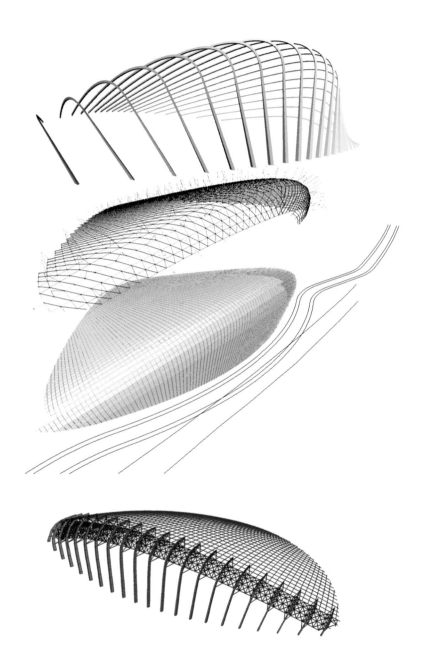

top left Exploded axonometric showing an early iteration of the structural layers: this hierarchy was later revised so that the glazing would sit between the gridshell and supporting ribs

bottom left Propped by the structural ribs, the north face of the Flower Dome is fully supported while the stiffened section at the 'nose' of the building works as an arch, and the shallow slope of the south façade (in red) continues to work as a gridshell: *"A pure gridshell is like an egg – strong until you put an uneven load on it, when it breaks. Which is why we've got two layers to the structure – the ribs, which resist the dynamic loads, and the gridshell, which supports the glass."* Paul Baker

above The two structural systems working in tandem in the Flower Dome

right Wilkinson Eyre's detail drawing and subcontractor's model showing the structural ribs connected by steel struts to the gridshell below

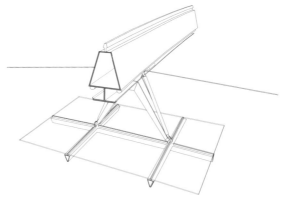

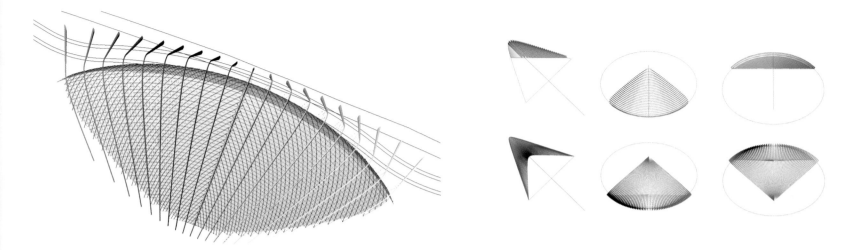

left Passers-by highlight the extraordinary scale of the waterfront marathon route, created in the space between gridshell and structural ribs on the Flower Dome's north façade: *"The idea of kicking the ribs forward came up at a workshop in Singapore. That was when we started talking about the amazing space we could create in between."* Matthew Potter

above Plan drawing and sketches developing the geometry of the structural ribs

Along the waterfront edge of the Flower Dome, the ribs separate from the gridshell beneath to support the inward tilt of this northern façade, framing a spectacular arcade along the waterfront. This public promenade was part of the competition brief, allowing the route of Singapore's annual marathon to follow the shoreline of Marina Bay. Although it was originally hoped that the ribs could be brought back in so that the whole form would tilt over in a gesture towards the bay, there was concern that they would not give the necessary support in this configuration, and so they were kicked out to create the promenade space.

Longitudinally, the geometry of the ribs influenced the final definition of the gridshell geometry below. Constructed from manufactured steel, the grid members also have a triangular section with the narrowest edge facing downwards. This allows the glazing units to be fixed from above while offering the least obstruction to daylight and the further benefit of giving the lightest possible appearance from below. However, in working through the precise setting out we found the effects of small misalignments between the uniform members as they follow the curved surface along each arc of the grid. This was dealt with by introducing a trapezoidal node piece, with a slightly larger profile than the grid members. This takes out the twisting effect of successive minor misalignments and also provides the necessary fabrication tolerances.

Working closely with Neil Thomas of Atelier One, each element was massaged into shape to reconcile the various structural, environmental and visual requirements. As the structural design developed, we repeatedly checked back to see how the visitor experience inside the biomes would be affected by the various options. The visual effect of the external ribs against the mesh of the gridshell was one concern. Our work moulding the forms reinforced the idea that having the ribs on the outside would not only stiffen the structure but also be less noticeable from the inside, and that visitors would start to read the gridshell rather than the ribs. We had done some work in this area before, developing proposals for an ethylene tetrafluoroethylene (or ETFE, a transparent polymer) roof for a large cricket ground in the UK. The focus was on preventing shadows onto the pitch because that would affect play, and similarly in Singapore we wanted to create an expression of sky without all the accompanying structure. From the outside, in contrast, the ribs make a strong visual impact. Although some critics have said the conservatories look over-structured, the reality is that as a team we fought incredibly hard to keep the structure as light as possible—to the extent that we had to have the local building codes changed because the British Standards (on which they are based) have a factor related to snow-loading which is irrelevant in Singapore.

The steel gridshell supports large double-glazed units that are key to the environmental modulation of the building, reinforcing our intent to achieve as much environmental control as possible through passive means before resorting to active systems. A characteristic of toroidal gridded surfaces is that when segmented from their axis of rotation, repetition of the shape of the sets of bays in the grid can be achieved. This led to economies in the sizing of glazing units and the grid members. The axis of rotation for each toroidal

above The Flower Dome's expanse of glazed gridshell as seen from the upper terrace: *"It's a pretty efficient structure. On the outside the ribs enhance the organic form of the conservatories, but on the inside you don't really read them. And that's all part of the trick."* Paul Baker

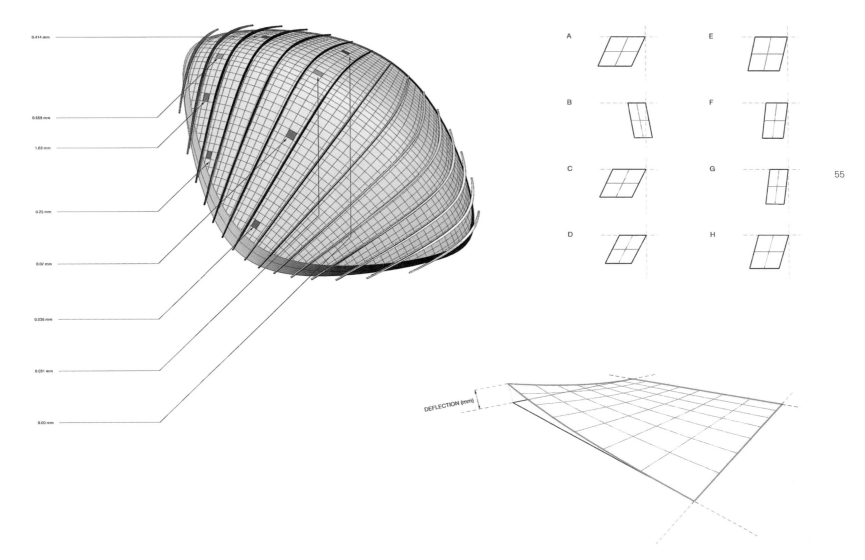

0.414 mm

0.668 mm

1.63 mm

0.25 mm

0.07 mm

0.036 mm

0.031 mm

0.00 mm

A

B

C

D

E

F

G

H

DEFLECTION (mm)

above Setting out diagrams for the glazing panels showing the incremental twist in the Cloud Forest's geometry

form was located some distance below ground, so that once a rim had been established for the overall form of each conservatory to sit on, the radial components of the structure (ribs and also the relevant gridshell members) would never fully converge at this rim. The geometry allowed for repeatability across the glazing units, and on the Flower Dome most have an average surface area of around six square metres, allowing each module to be lifted and manoeuvred easily.

Distorting the Cloud Forest geometry introduced a level of complexity: a much greater number of unique shapes of glass would be required to tile the envelope and, by compressing the form in one direction only, a certain degree of 'twist' was introduced to the geometry. The gridshell mullions were now required to twist along their length in response to the changed form and the panes of glass themselves became non-planar. These issues were resolved comparatively simply by keeping the individual mullions straight. The slight oversizing of the connecting node mentioned previously was sufficient to accommodate the incremental rotation and take out the twist.

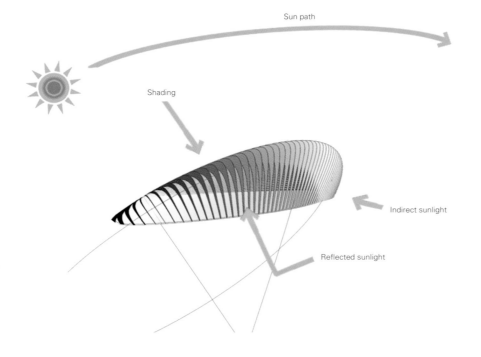

Sun path

Shading

Indirect sunlight

Reflected sunlight

left Sunpath diagram showing the effect of direct, indirect and deflected sunlight on the Flower Dome

bottom Sequence showing incremental reduction of solar gain: *"We did a simple mock-up of the glazing on site, just a horizontal unit with no walls. When you walked underneath the glass it was like walking into the shade, it was such a dramatic temperature shift. It was the best demonstration for me that the glass really was going to work."* Paul Baker

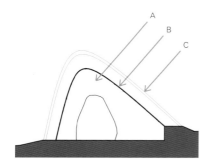

1. No shades

A = 374 w/M2
B = 936 w/M2
C = 1040 w/M2

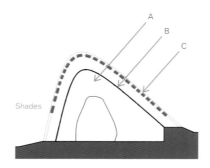

2. Partially deployed shades

A = 260 w/M2
B = 650 w/M2
C = 1040 w/M2

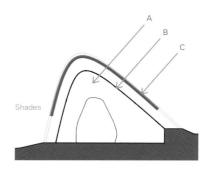

3. Completely deployed shades

A = 40 w/M2
B = 100 w/M2
C = 1040 w/M2

above Flower Dome interior with the sunshading deployed

Although we debated using various combinations of ETFE and glass, glass was chosen early on because, with a high performance low-e coating (impossible to apply to ETFE) on the inner surface, a significant amount of heat gain could be prevented. The glazing therefore has a very high visual light transmission of 64% coupled with a very low solar heat gain coefficient of 38%.

The steel ribs of the superstructure house a fabric sunshading system which helps prevent the buildings from overheating in periods of direct sunlight. The shading system is concealed in reveals within the ribs and its mechanism is based on yacht roller-reefing. We did a large amount of work to develop the shading solution, at first exploring the idea that the ribs themselves might be a way of cutting out the low level sun, acting like gigantic louvres. However, it soon became clear that a more sensitive system would be needed.

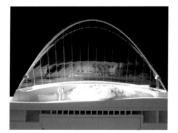

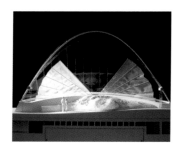

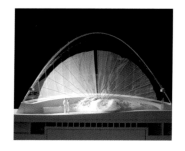

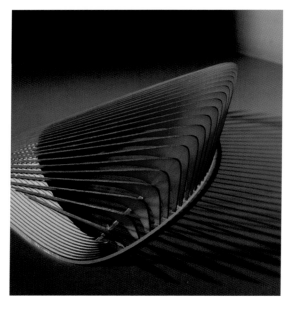

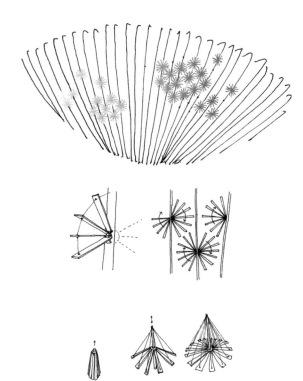

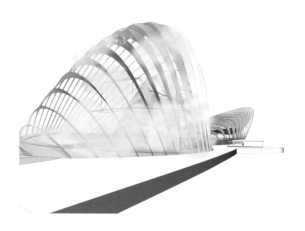

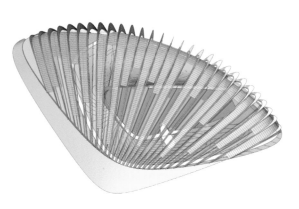

top left Fan-like fabric sunshading on the Davies Alpine House

top middle Early models suggested that sufficient shading might be achieved using the structural ribs as a series of giant louvres

top right Suggested shading option with flower-like umbrellas

bottom left More shading experiments with atmospheric mist and radial shutter blinds

With the gridshell stabilised and the scale of the glazing mullions reduced, we looked at placing retractable shading on the ribs so that the process of shading the conservatories might become an event in itself—again informed by Wilkinson Eyre's experience on the Davies Alpine House, which uses fan-like structures to shade the space within.

Many of the ideas investigated were highly creative— huge fans unfolding across the space, origami structures spinning out and opening, little umbrellas flowering over the whole surface, and even artificial clouds using water from Marina Bay. The final solution reached was roller-reefing in a geometry reminiscent of pineapples or pine cones, which provides a dramatic spectacle in use. Throughout the day, light and temperature readings are taken within the conservatories to determine where shade is needed, and computer-controlled motors unfurl the polyester sail fabric shades in response. Different zones within the conservatories can also be shaded specifically to suit the requirements of the planting within.

above Drawing of the final shading solution based on yacht roller-reefing, seen here unfurled at the Flower Dome: *"The conservatories have a responsive structure to suit the fact that Singapore's climate can change so much in the space of a single day."* Paul Baker

right Plan and section of a structural bay showing the sunshading to the Cloud Forest (left) and the Flower Dome (right)

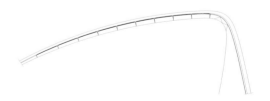

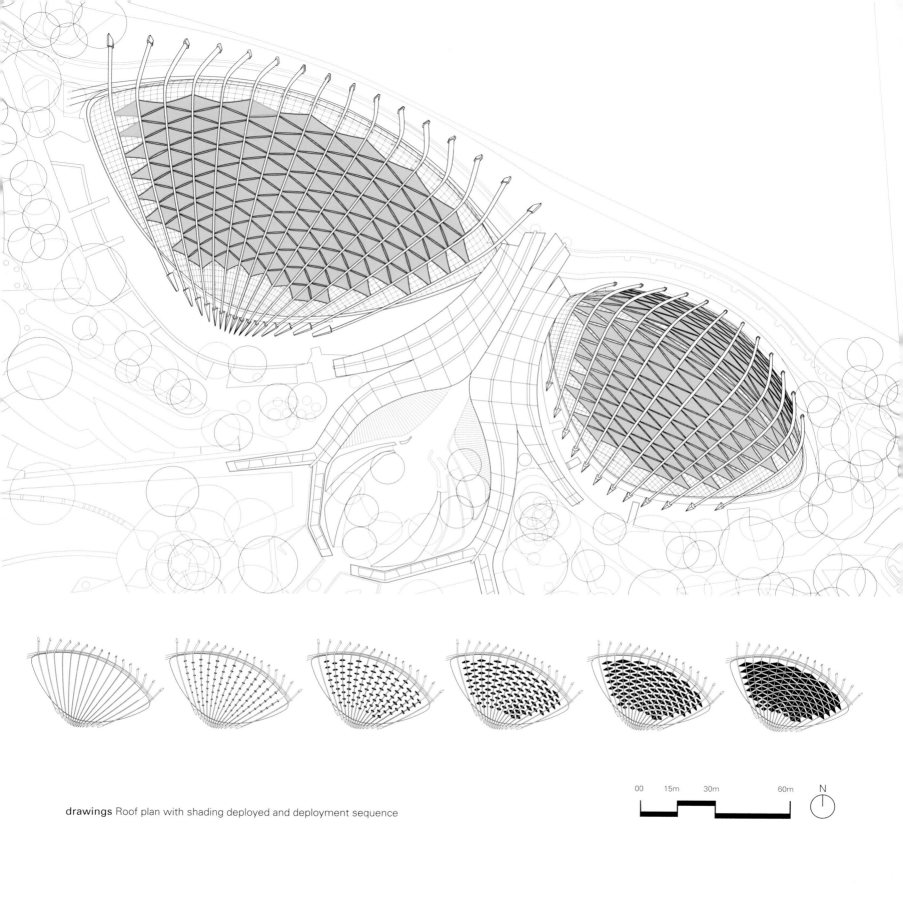

drawings Roof plan with shading deployed and deployment sequence

00   15m   30m   60m

N

above Aerial view showing
shading deployed

left The interior of the Climatron, St Louis, inspired by Buckminster Fuller

right The Palm House at the Royal Botanic Gardens, Kew

Nature's balance

Patrick Bellew
Director, Atelier Ten

We were fortunate when embarking on the competition design for Gardens by the Bay to have some prior experience with the exacting environmental requirements of glasshouses through an eight-year involvement with the Royal Botanic Gardens at Kew. In that time we designed and constructed the Davies Alpine House with Wilkinson Eyre and through that project had come to understand the balance between daylight, sunlight and heat that is essential to the survival of the plants and to the comfort of visitors.

Most of the glasshouses that we are familiar with, the Palm House at Kew for example, were designed to maximise light and solar gain to emulate hot, humid or arid conditions in cool or temperate climates. The 'Climatron' at the Botanical Gardens in St Louis (1960) was perhaps the first air-conditioned glasshouse in the world and, inspired by Buckminster Fuller, the designers used innovative façade and conditioning systems to deliver a striking and effective building.

At Gardens by the Bay, the climate of Singapore multiplied the environmental challenges and the scale of the buildings amplified them further. Singapore is always hot and humid: it is just a few miles from the equator and so receives intense sunlight from all sides, but it is also frequently cloudy and light levels are often poor for several days at a time.

The braced gridshell structure with the high-performance, selectively coated glass and external shading came about following a great deal of analysis, conversation and negotiation within the design team in order to optimise the combination and to ensure that the plants received adequate daylight without excess solar gain. The conditioning system is required both to remove heat gains from solar and other sources and to provide air movement around the plants and the people. All of the pathways around the building are cooled by underfloor cooling and a displacement conditioning system provides cool air into the occupied zone through several hundred integrated diffusers and 'bins' in the structure and landscape beds.

The air dehumidification and cooling process is part of a larger system that generates electricity, heat and cooling from a renewable source powered by timber thinnings from Singapore's tree management programme. Air is dehumidified using desiccants in liquid form. These absorb moisture from the incoming air and are then 'dried' by heating with waste heat from the biomass plant. The chilled water is also generated from the waste energy stream through absorption chillers. The net effect is a zero-carbon conditioning system for the two glasshouses.

The successful fusion of architecture and technology at Gardens by the Bay is very much a result of the close and open working relationship between the client and design team and within the design team itself. It was a technically challenging undertaking, anything but straightforward, but it was never less than exhilarating and the resulting buildings are, to say the least, astonishing.

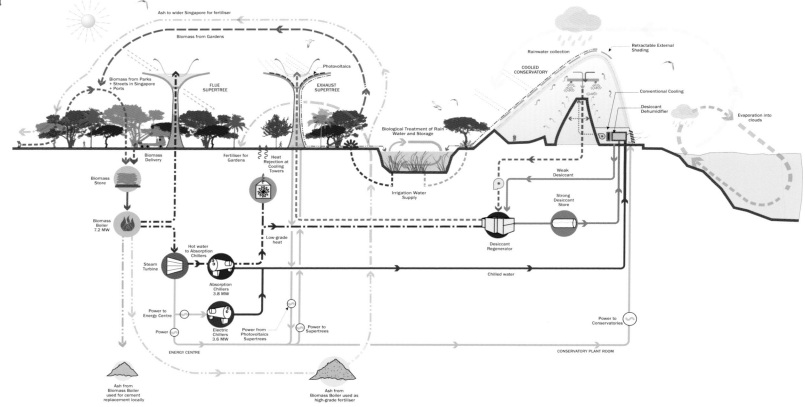

Ash to wider Singapore for fertiliser

Biomass from Gardens

Rainwater collection

Retractable External Shading

COOLED CONSERVATORY

Biomass from Parks + Streets in Singapore + Ports

FLUE SUPERTREE

Photovoltaics

EXHAUST SUPERTREE

Conventional Cooling

Desiccant Dehumidifier

Biological Treatment of Rain Water and Storage

Evaporation into clouds

Biomass Delivery

Fertiliser for Gardens

Heat Rejection at Cooling Towers

Weak Desiccant

Biomass Store

Irrigation Water Supply

Strong Desiccant Store

Biomass Boiler 7.2 MW

Low-grade heat

Desiccant Regenerator

Hot water to Absorption Chillers

Steam Turbine

Absorption Chillers 3.8 MW

Chilled water

Power to Energy Centre

Power

Electric Chillers 3.6 MW

Power from Photovoltaics Supertrees

Power to Supertrees

Power to Conservatories

ENERGY CENTRE

CONSERVATORY PLANT ROOM

Ash from Biomass Boiler used for cement replacement locally

Ash from Biomass Boiler used as high-grade fertiliser

The environmental story

left Atelier Ten's diagram showing the garden's 'internal' ecosystem, linking the main structures on the Gardens by the Bay site: *"The diagram shows that the conservatories don't just sap energy and resource out of Singapore. Instead it's about them having a symbiotic relationship with the gardens. It's the idea of nature being balanced."* Paul Baker

below Diagrams – again by Atelier Ten – showing the passive environmental system at the Davies Alpine House, Kew

The environmental approach adopted at the Bay South garden is based around the idea that nature itself holds the key to sustainable development. As in nature, each built element within the gardens is part of a wider ecosystem, conceived by Atelier Ten, in which the main structures and planting work together symbiotically, simulating nature at work and minimising environmental impact. The environmental story for the conservatories themselves sits within the context of this wider system, as well as the client's brief for the specific growing requirements within. They are designed to achieve as much environmental control as possible through passive means—drawing on the fundamental strategies of traditional colonial architecture, where simple principles of shading and ventilation help to cool the space— before resorting to highly efficient, active systems. Although the conservatories could be seen as 'alien' to the natural setting of the gardens, they do not sap their surroundings of energy and resource—they simply capture the landscape below them, modifying nature to create new growing environments. They provide the context to our design story: the creation of a 'supernature'.

The principal design challenge in both biomes is addressing the conflicting need to maintain the high light levels required by the plants whilst minimising the associated solar heat gain, and we once again looked to our collaboration with Atelier Ten at the Davies Alpine House at Kew in developing the passive environmental strategy. Both buildings represent a careful balance between light and heat: while traditional glasshouses trap the light and heat of the sun, the biomes modify this process through responsive design, allowing the necessary daylight for plant growth without overheating the space within. The Alpine House achieves this by using an underground labyrinth—inspired by the physical principles of termite mounds—which provides cool air to the plants, coupled with a relatively tall internal space which creates a stack effect to draw warmed air out of the building. Like the Alpine House, the Singapore biomes are optimised environmentally by containing a large volume within a relatively small surface area. In addition, the form of the Flower Dome is tilted forward so that it leans over towards Marina Bay. The north façade is therefore self-shaded and never receives the full glare of the sun.

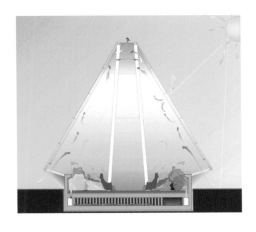

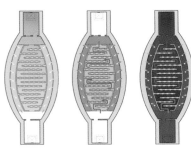

The plants inside the Flower Dome demanded a 'perpetual spring', a false season which would fool them into unnatural planting cycles to suit the displays. To create this repeated spring, we had to drop the temperature inside the conservatory and it became clear early in the design process that the best time to do this would be during the evening when the environmental systems would not be fighting the heat of the day. We had real concerns that the steel structure would struggle to adapt to these vast differences in temperature, shrinking and changing shape continually. When the environmental team began to carry out their computational fluid dynamics (CFD) modelling, however, we realised that the temperature at the top of both conservatories would not alter very much when the forced temperature changes were made to the plants at the bottom. The air stratifies so that although there is a big pocket of hot air at the top, the effect of thermal expansion on the overall structure is not too dramatic. With this realisation, the design became much more straightforward—both structurally and environmentally. This stratification of air is key to how the conservatories work: only the base of the volume needs to be cooled. The envelope is critical to the success of the system: the structure has been designed to cast as little shadow as possible while highly selective glass is used to filter out as much heat as possible, as described elsewhere in this book. When the sun comes out, deployable shades are used to control the light levels and limit the heat gain.

In the Flower Dome, the main displays act as a bowl where the cool air is held, while warmer air rises naturally to the upper part of the glasshouse where it collects and stratifies. The higher structures and terraces such as the baobab 'leaf' are contained by low balustrades in order to prevent the cool air trickling off them. Where necessary, displacement ventilation tubes have been introduced to feed cold air onto the plants at low velocity—just as at the Alpine House, albeit at a vastly different scale. Fundamentally, the Cloud Forest works in the same way, but required a slightly different approach. The central mountain structure meant that

visitors would potentially get hotter as they went up it, which was obviously contradictory to a similar experience in nature. So the entire mountain has been made into a giant air displacement unit. Cold air spills out of the holes and trickles down the mountain so both plants and people are kept cool efficiently. There were concerns that when visitors moved away from the mountain on the aerial walkways they would move into pockets of uncomfortably hot air, but the fogger sprays introduced to create the atmospheric mist typical of tropical montane climates dampen the air sufficiently to mitigate this. In contrast, the central hub is an unconditioned, open air space, with the structure and form of the sheltering canopy designed to maximise natural air movement throughout.

Fittingly, the primary source of energy for cooling the conservatories is biomass. NParks collect around 70 tons of cuttings each day from the famous rain trees that line the streets of Singapore, clearing the internal branches to allow for air and light, and maintaining the canopy for shade. It is therefore plants themselves that are used to help create the cool environment needed for these Mediterranean and montane 'visitors' to survive. The biomass boiler is part of a CCHP system, powering absorption chillers that convert the generated heat to chilled water. This is fed to the conservatories for use in cooling the fabric, lowering the temperature of all the concrete paths. The power generated is used to run the conventional chillers in the plant rooms. Here, fresh air is drawn in and dried with a desiccant prior to passing through the chillers for delivery onto the planted displays. The desiccant reduces the amount of energy required to cool the air but itself becomes saturated with extracted moisture. The hot air collected from the top of the glasshouses is used to regenerate the desiccant by driving off the moisture.

right Fogger sprays in the Cloud Forest create a cooling atmospheric mist around the central mountain structure

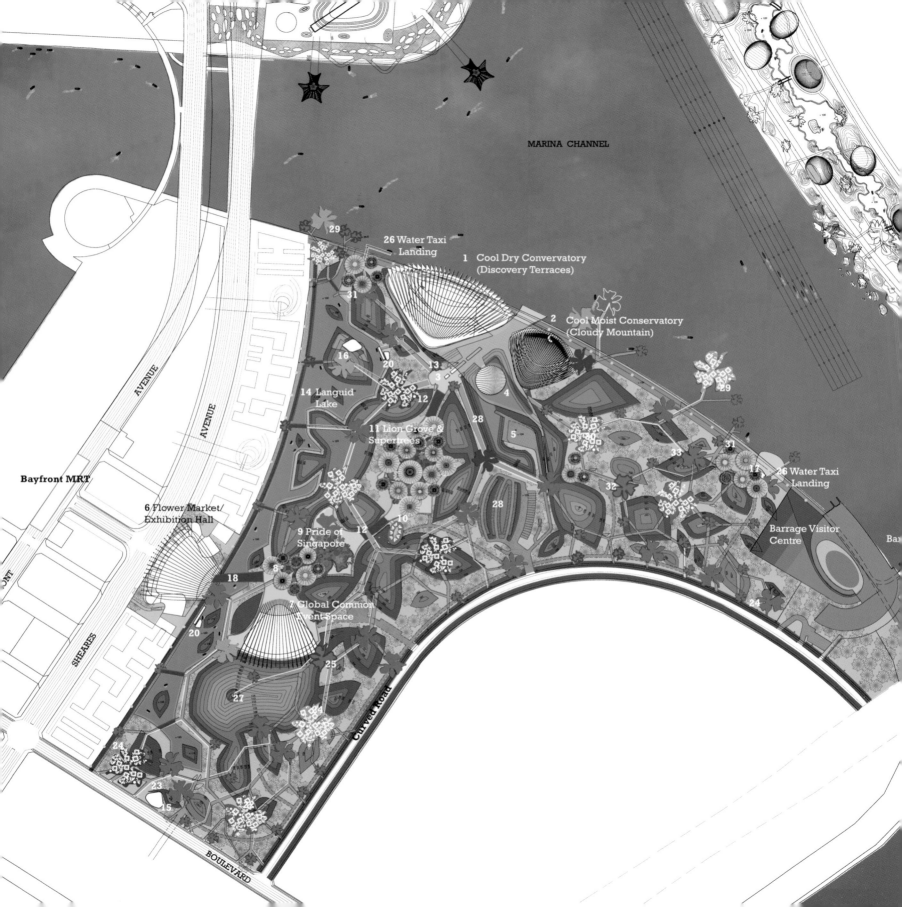

MARINA CHANNEL

Bayfront MRT

AVENUE

AVENUE

SHEARES

BOULEVARD

Curved Road

29

26 Water Taxi
Landing

1 Cool Dry Convervatory
(Discovery Terraces)

2 Cool Moist Conservatory
(Cloudy Mountain)

31

16

20

13

3

12

14 Languid
Lake

4

28

5

11 Lion Grove &
Supertrees

29

31

6 Flower Market/
Exhibition Hall

9 Pride of
Singapore

12

10

28

32

11

26 Water Taxi
Landing

Barrage Visitor
Centre

Ba

8

18

7 Global Common
Event Space

25

24

20

27

4

23

15

24

Authoring the landscape

Andrew Grant
Director, Grant Associates

left Andrew Grant's
competition masterplan for
the Bay South gardens

From outside the glasshouses are striking architectural landmarks in a landscape setting. Internally, however, it is the plants that take centre stage, set off by the sweeping forms and immense scale of the glasshouse shells. The interior landscape strategy creates two contrasting experiences and internal environments. The Flower Dome is a 'Theatre of Plants' with the emphasis on the colours and flowers of the Mediterranean world whilst the Cloud Forest is an immersive vertical journey through a tropical montane cloud forest.

Each conservatory is organised around a principal route that navigates through the space as a gently ramping spine with a series of offset gardens and secondary pathways. The Flower Dome is arranged as a series of leaf-like terraces linked to this main spine. These display plants from specific regions of the world including Chile, the Mediterranean, South Africa, California, Western Australia and Madagascar. The Cloud Forest is more of a collection of three-dimensional spaces integrating the experiences associated with a cloud forest—including a waterfall, ravine, a lost world and mountainside. The layers of the forest are experienced from suspended and elevated pathways that navigate through the space offering extra drama to the journey.

The coordination of landscape and horticultural needs with those of the structural and environmental engineering has been a feature of the design process. Reconciling the impact of plants, soil depths and drainage with structural loadings, cool air distribution ducting and diffusers, general maintenance and operational needs required detailed collaboration. In addition, the innovations in planting techniques, especially on the Cloud Forest mountain, were possible only through collaboration with the client's specialist horticulturists, irrigation designers and the planting contractor.

Although plants are the main focus of the project, the conservatories are not just about botanical collections but are enriched with other functions and experiences. The Flower Dome houses a number of function spaces and restaurants which take advantage of the dramatic botanical setting whilst the Cloud Forest integrates leading-edge multimedia interpretation to reinforce the educational background to the project. At night, each conservatory transforms into a magical landscape, offering an entirely different display and experience of plants and space.

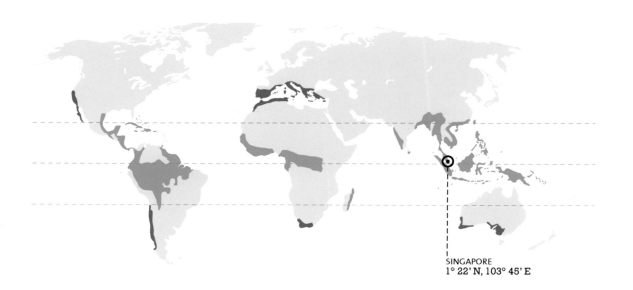

left Diagrams showing the
basic narrative principle
behind the conservatory
planting, with the
cool-dry Flower Dome
showcasing plants from
the Mediterranean climate
zones and the cool-moist
Cloud Forest those from
tropical montane regions,
highlighting the threats of
climate change on natural
biodiversity in these areas

SINGAPORE
1° 22' N, 103° 45' E

right Wilkinson Eyre's sectional diagrams of the Flower Dome and Cloud Forest with Grant Associates' overlay showing the layering of planting within

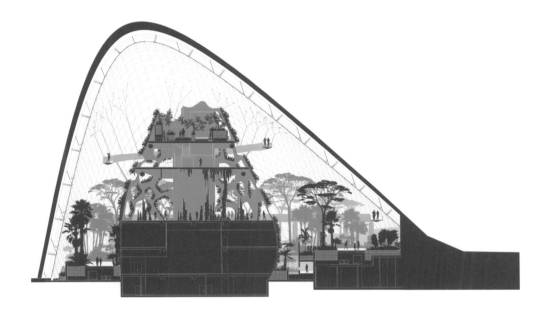

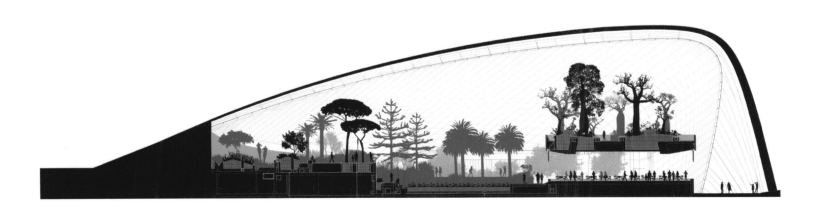

Flower Dome

left Visitors enjoy the cool, dry environment within the Flower Dome: *"Dining outside is a big feature of life in the Mediterranean – but nobody in Singapore can do it as it's just too hot. So that was exactly the kind of opportunity we wanted to create in the Flower Dome."* Paul Baker

The Flower Dome tells the story of plants and people in the Mediterranean climate zone, and how plants cultivated in these regions will gradually become endangered as global temperatures rise. It has a planted footprint of more than 10,100 square metres under glass and, through a cycle of regularly refreshed planting in the central Flower Field, aims to bring alive the experience of seasonal change for visitors more used to Singapore's eternally tropical climate and lush green vegetation. Envisaged as a 'valley' in contrast to the mountain of the adjacent Cloud Forest, the landform draws inspiration from Mediterranean landscapes, evoking the language of dry hillsides punctuated with rocky terraces and stony outcrops, and exploring the intimate bond between land, geology, vegetation and cultivation.

Visitors enter from the central hub, passing into an intentionally compressed and dark entrance space. A short ramp draws visitors away from the doors and towards a viewpoint, releasing them into the daylight to view a wide panorama across the internal landscape of the conservatory. In the centre of the space is the vast Flower Field, with its seasonally changing display of flowers. A gently sloping route leads visitors down through a series of gardens from Mediterranean climate zones around the globe, each with their own network of paths, interpretation and seating areas. Walls behind the terraces of planting are painted rich earth tones to accentuate the colour and diversity of the plants.

Although during the competition stage we focused on trying to keep the sun out of this cool dry conservatory, the final planting brief established the need for as much daylight as possible, but with heat gain carefully controlled. Initially the planting displays were designed like shelves around the central hollow of the Flower Field, but this would have created too much shade. In order to get direct sunlight to as much of the planting as possible, we designed two huge, leaf-like platforms which in plan 'hug' the central field. The larger leaf, to the eastern end of the conservatory and adjacent to the hub, supports an extraordinary plantation of baobabs, bottle trees and cacti. The large event space below is enclosed by glazing, with views across the Flower Field and out to the bay. A smaller leaf, to the western end, supports a Californian garden, with views back across the conservatory and sheltering chef Jason Atherton's Pollen restaurant below. This strategy of raised 'leaves' allows direct sunlight to reach the planting, and maximises the benefits of air stratification within the conservatory, whilst creating considerable areas of dining and event space underneath. The requirement for a large hospitality space developed in ambition throughout the project as it became clear how attractive a space the Flower Dome would be for visitors. Large events such as the World Orchid Conference, parties and exhibitions can be accommodated with ease because the internal climate is so comfortable compared to the heat outside.

74

1 Californian garden
2 Pollen restaurant
3 Olive Grove
4 Flower Field
5 Flower Dome event space
6 Baobabs
7 Hub / Canopy
8 Australian garden
9 Marathon route
10 Plant room

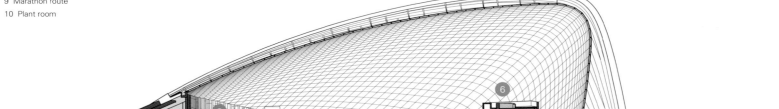

drawing Cross section through Flower Dome

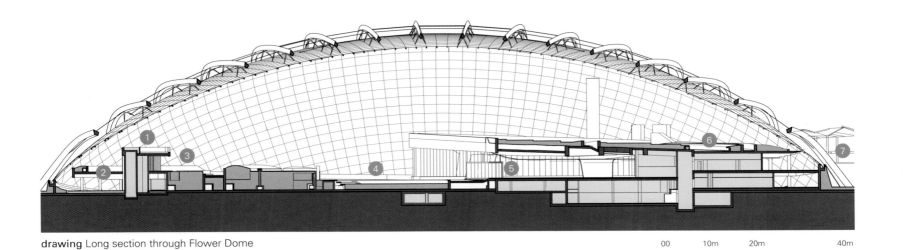

drawing Long section through Flower Dome

00   10m   20m   40m

Cloud Forest

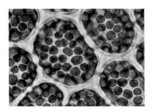

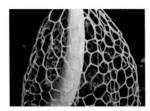

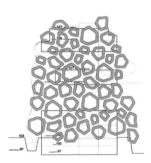

above Cell structures and the delicate filigree of the stinkhorn mushroom informed the abstract structure of the mountain

left View of the mountain and waterfall from the Cloud Forest entrance

With a smaller footprint but greater height than the Flower Dome, the Cloud Forest has at its heart a planted mountain that contrasts strongly with the broad vistas of its sister conservatory. This biome highlights the relationship between plants and the planet, showing how the warming of the cool tropical cloud forests will threaten biodiversity. The mountain was part of our earliest concept for the conservatories. In essence, it is a 'dressed' building, a simple, abstract structure which forms a neat duality with the valley of the Flower Dome. However, it also has a purpose—not only does it provide exhibition space within, it also acts as a huge air displacement unit to help cool the conservatory. Because of this, it is designed as an open, cell-like structure, based on examples in nature such as the delicate, filigree 'bridal veil' of the stinkhorn mushroom. It was carefully modelled to see how it would work in terms of construction and planting, and we explored a number of solutions such as creating a skin of pre-planted hoops, although the design eventually had to be adapted to suit the construction techniques available. The final structure is therefore shuttered concrete, which was then covered in planting.

The entrance to the Cloud Forest is at the lower level of the central hub to maximise the impact of the conservatory's height. In contrast to the Flower Dome, where visitors are free to wander as they please, the design of the Cloud Forest is such that visitors follow a distinct route. They enter the space at the bottom of the waterfall—which, dropping 35 metres from the mountain structure, is the tallest indoor waterfall in the world. From this initial orientation space, a path leads up and around the mountain, with views into a plant-filled ravine below. A lift then takes visitors up to a level just short of the top of the mountain. There is a short climb to the Lost World at the summit, which has a reflective pool surrounded by specialist high-altitude plants such as the infamous Venus flytrap.

Visitors can experience the forest at different levels from the walkways that loop out from the mountain. The highest of these, the vertiginous Cloud Walk, brings visitors out and around the space, while the lower Treetop Walk provides a winding route through the vegetation at canopy level. From time to time, as the visitors explore these walkways, the space fills with mist. These frequent—and necessary—changes of atmosphere within both conservatories provide a unique spectacle. In the Cloud Forest, everyone stops to watch the place descend into a mysterious gloom when the foggers are turned on, while in the Flower Field, the silent, gradual unfurling of the sunshades overhead is a little like a giant cloud passing over, casting huge shadows over the displays within.

From the walkways, visitors descend through the Cloud Forest mountain through a series of exhibitions, including a display of epiphytic plants and a cave-like space with Dr Tan's collection of stalactites known as the Crystal Mountain. Further down, a large exhibit describes the impact of incremental temperature change on the world's climate and the sustainable technologies employed at Gardens by the Bay. On leaving the mountain, a loop at the lowest level leads through a secret, fern-filled garden. This dark, misty and mysterious place—the Ravine—emphasises the contrast between the two conservatories. While the Flower Dome is all rich, earthy tones, the planted language of the Cloud Forest is a green jungle, pinpointed with flashes of colour.

1 Crystal Mountain exhibition
2 Lost World
3 Forest Walk
4 Cloud Walk
5 Treetop Walk
6 Plant room
7 Ravine
8 Marathon route

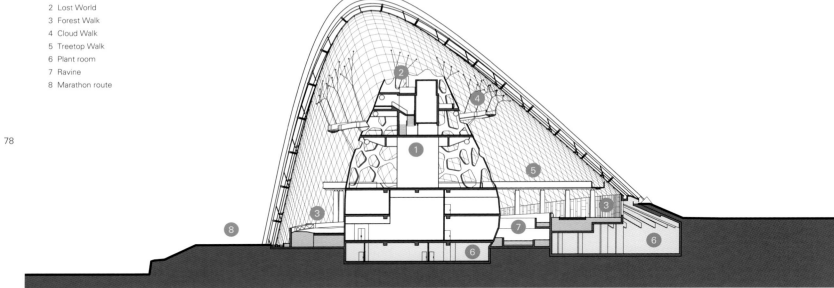

drawing Cloud Forest cross section

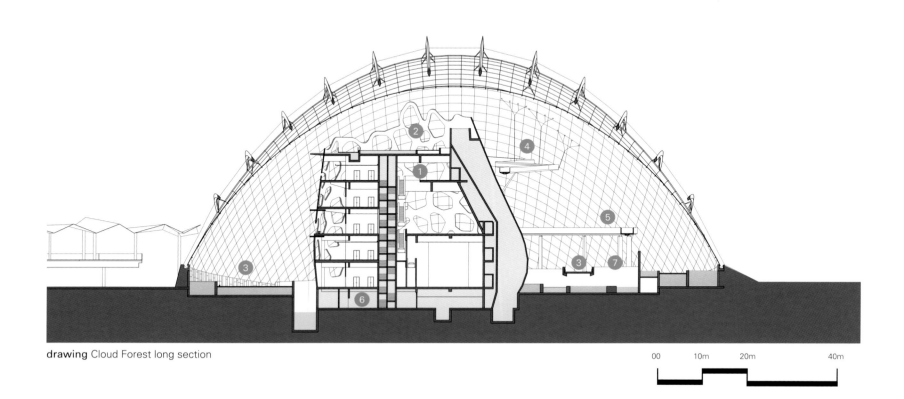

drawing Cloud Forest long section

00   10m   20m   40m

The hub

The hub space that sits between the two conservatories is vital to the visitor experience, and is in effect the central point from which the Grant Associates masterplan grows. From this point, the 'epiphytic' paths identified in the original conceptual diagram creep out across the gardens, drawing visitors in as well as leading them out to explore. The hub serves a number of pragmatic functions—ticketing, wayfinding, orientation, retail—but also sets the scene for the experience to follow. It is a prelude to the biomes: a warm-up space before the big reveal, dark and shady to provide a contrast to the bright daylight of the conservatories.

At the competition stage, the hub was identified as in internal space (in fact at this point we also had a third support biome), but the team felt that this would lessen the drama of entering the conservatories. We were interested in the idea of accentuating the difference between inside and outside, and wanted to create a shock when people entered the cooled spaces rather than having it mitigated by a conditioned hub area outside. The hub was therefore designed as a counterpoint to the conservatories. It is an outdoor space rather than a building, naturally ventilated and with individual pavilions protected from the elements by a large canopy. This shelter is made up of a series of smaller, oversailing canopies that extend far out into

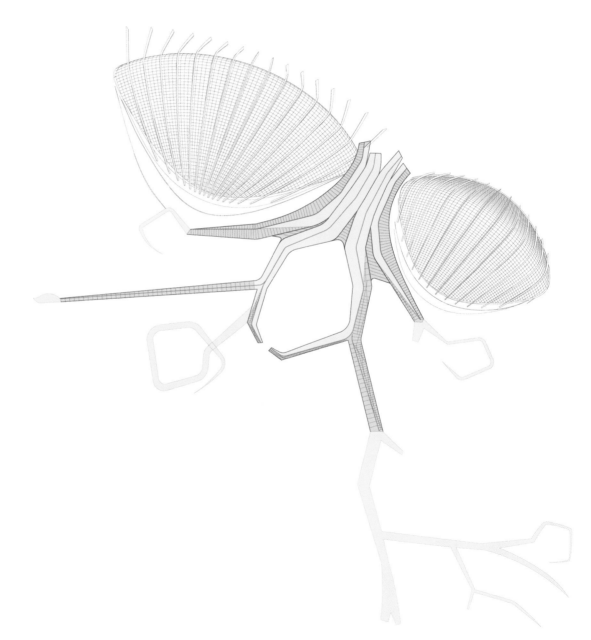

far left Sketch models showing the development of the hub canopy

left Plan showing the canopy structure extending out into the gardens from the hub

below Sketch and image showing the hub sitting in the 'cleavage' between the two biomes: *"The hub became a key interface between the modulated environments of the conservatories and the outdoors."* Matthew Potter

the gardens. They reinforce the circulation routes of the masterplan, with the architectural language of pavilions and canopy gradually breaking down the further they are from the hub, with the solid roof gradually becoming transparent, then transforming into a planted pergola before disappearing completely. The canopies converge at the hub point in an articulated surface which expresses the elements coming together. Daylight filters in through the gaps where the different layers of canopy oversail, and through sections of coloured glass. This considerable area of sheltered space creates a shady and comfortable environment for visitors to meet, rest and shop using ideas from traditional colonial architecture: the canopy funnels breezes coming off the bay, with additional cooling provided by ceiling fans.

The hub works at two levels, reinforcing the topography that Grant Associates created on this flat, reclaimed site. The ground is built up over the back of the two glasshouses to bring visitors to the upper level, which connects directly to the gardens beyond. Here people arrive, buy tickets and orient themselves, in what is still essentially an outdoor space. The lower hub level is more building-like: here are the back of house spaces and a service road, all covered by the planting above, and for the public a series of shops and cafés which link directly to the waterfront promenade. A significant

consideration in the design of the hub was how to deal with the edge condition between the conservatories (the Flower Dome in particular) and the ramp that leads up to the raised space between them—a key interface between the modulated environment and the outdoors. This involved ensuring that the geometry of the structure could still be read, as well as allowing for the collection of water drain-off and the distribution of air into the internal spaces.

With its two levels, the hub architecture plays an important part in determining the visitor experience, emphasising through light, temperature and level changes the differences not just between inside and outside, but also between the two biomes themselves. The entrance to the Flower Dome is from the hub's upper level, a short ramp drawing visitors up to admire the spectacular panorama of planted terraces, while the Cloud Forest is accessed from the lower level. The arrangement is the result of many discussions about how visitors should move around the biomes, how they should arrive, and where they were led. Although it is possible for NParks to usher visitors into whichever of the biomes is emptier, the hub does set up a sequential route with the entrance to the Flower Dome at the same level as the ticket office and its exit opposite the entrance to the Cloud Forest.

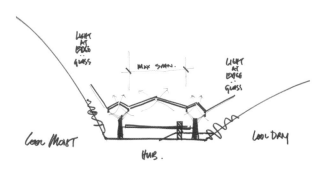

left Elevational drawing of the 50-metre supertree

right View from the walkway connecting the main supertrees

Supertree

The grove of twelve 'supertrees' which form the backdrop to the cooled conservatories were primarily the design responsibility of Grant Associates and Atelier One. Constructed from steel and planted with vertical gardens, they are striking visual statement as well as forming a vital part of the wider environmental infrastructure that allows the conservatories to function.

Wilkinson Eyre was closely involved with the design of the largest of the supertree structures. The core was developed with an internal escape stair and an external stair that winds up through the planting with a laser-cut Corten steel balustrade. At the top, 50 metres from the ground, there is an external walkway around a two-level space with kitchens on the lower level and a spectacular public bar above.

left View from the supertrees towards the Cloud Forest

near right Detail of the laser-cut steel sunshade

far right The supertrees in context

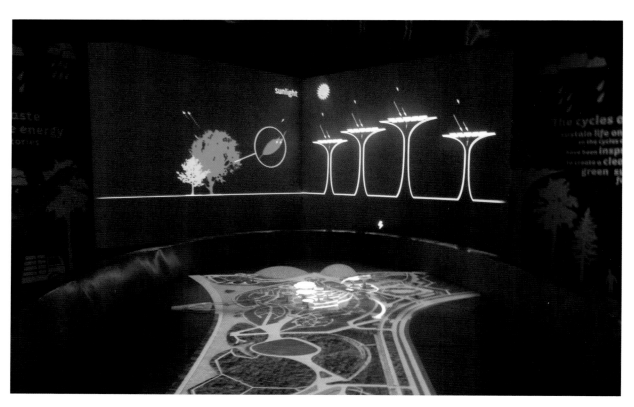

opposite page Sequence from Land Design's audio-visual display in the depths of the Cloud Forest's mountain

left Audio visual display showing the environmental solutions employed at Gardens by the Bay: *"We wanted to do more than just satisfy the brief. We wanted to extend the visitor experience and demonstrate the workings of the building and put climate change on the agenda."* Paul Baker

below far left Andrew Grant's conceptual sketch showing routes around the mountain

below left Diagram showing refinement of these routes

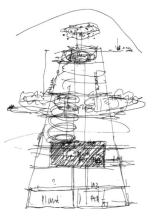

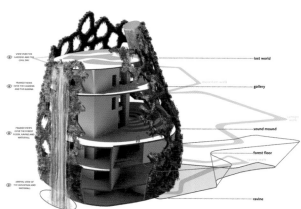

A visitor's eye view

Peter Higgins
Creative Director, Land Design Studio

As experiential designers, it is familiar territory for us [Land Design Studio] to work with Wilkinson Eyre in cultural spaces, and it is always an enjoyable collaborative journey as they understand the sensitive and integrated relationship between the narrative experience and the architectural enclosure.

The two conservatories at Gardens by the Bay had apparently very different imperatives to our familiar debate concerning the 'inside out' process as their primary function was to maximise the light ingress. As the concept progressed there was a fascinating irony with the advent of the mountain in the Cloud Forest. This welcome guest, a building within a building that would ultimately provide controlled lighting and movement systems, enabling us to tell our stories in a compelling and powerful way as well as conveniently providing a home for Dr Tan's fascinating stalactites.

In contrast, the equally elegant cool dry Flower Dome is less complex. It encourages a much lighter touch for our storytelling, which here attempts to interpret and inform in a discreet yet complementary manner, though the thresholds of entry and exit are marked by powerful graphic installations.

Gardens by the Bay represented a rare opportunity to design structures that work on many different levels—as city landmarks, as a major component of a spectacular landscape masterplan, as aesthetically pleasing objects, and as a vehicle for innovative environmental and structural engineering. At the same time they provide a purpose-built home for non-indigenous plants to be enjoyed by our visitors who are able to engage with informal learning programmes.

On reflection, our task has been to exploit many forms of communication media to help unlock the compelling stories that have been generously enabled within these visual and sensory spectacles. Hopefully some of our visitors will become knowledgeable ambassadors, celebrating horticultures and biodiversity and raising awareness of important global issues such as water and energy management as they travel on their way.

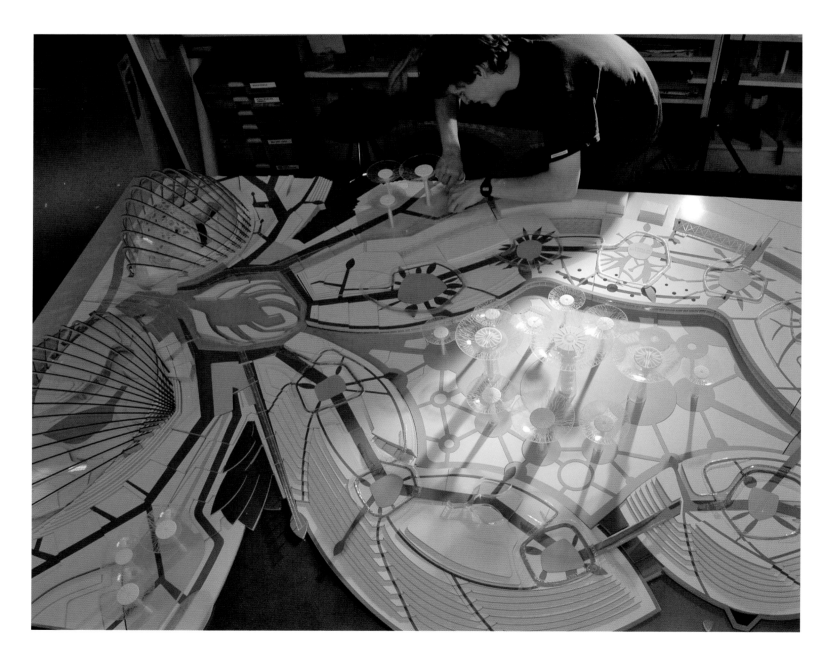

Modelmaking

left Wilkinson Eyre's Owen Rutter works on a preliminary model for the conservatory complex and grove of supertrees at Bay South

right Sketch models experimenting with the form and internal architecture of the conservatories

As with most Wilkinson Eyre projects, physical modelmaking formed an integral part of the design process as a means of both experimentation and presentation. By choosing not to take a fixed approach, the modelmakers on this project were able to experiment with the visual impact of a wide variety of materials—wood, wire, card and acrylic—in conveying the spirit of the scheme, as well as learning about their inherent qualities and tolerance when translated into models of varying scales.

The first model was made as part of the competition entry by Network Modelmakers. A huge piece showing concepts for all three Gardens by the Bay, it offered us an opportunity to set the tone for the entire project, so rather than building a traditional architectural model, the team took a more expressionistic approach, using colour and abstraction to convey their vision, ideas and enthusiasm for the scheme. Wilkinson Eyre's in-house modelmakers did a number of experiments with different techniques—especially for the structures—which were then adopted for the competition model. It was decided to use coloured acrylic over a printed underlay for a visually strong, stimulating effect, with the city and surrounding developments made from simple extruded blocks rather than anything more detailed.

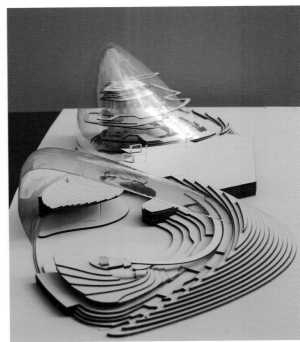

92

Having won the competition, modelmaking activity became focused on specific structures, with the team initially experimenting with various techniques to see how the conservatory design would work. In these early days, we made a number of study models from layered foamboard covered with plaster. Although sketchy, they helped us to agree the basic forms, refining the tilt on the Flower Dome to respond to the maximum angle of the sun. As the architectural team began work on the resolution of the structural design, the modelmakers concentrated on vac-forming shapes that would represent the two domes on larger scale models. A huge, heavy-duty MDF form was made in Sheffield by a company with a five-axis machine that worked a solid reduction process, eating away at the material to create a solid, three-dimensional object. The in-house team then used a facility closer to home to vac-form over the mould in plastic.

The vac-formed shapes were used on two fully layered, large scale models made during the concept design stages. These retained the abstract, colourful approach adopted for the competition model, but with the built elements of the gardens more fully worked. One went to the clients in Singapore for use in fundraising and

promotional activities, and the other was exhibited in the Royal Academy of Arts Summer Exhibition in London in 2008. All the large models were quite similar in feel, using unusual materials such as acrylics, because the project was so different, creative and abstract—and in many ways less 'architectural' than others produced by the modelshop.

Modelmaking was used for illustrative and presentation purposes but also for working things out. Alongside the larger site models, we created hundreds of study models to work out how different elements of the scheme would look, and to resolve specific architectural problems such as how the structural ribs of the conservatories would meet the ground. Modelling the interior of the Cloud Forest was a particular challenge, working out how the walkways would sit between the central mountain and the external gridshell. Even at this scale, the models showed the vast scale of the internal space, reassuring us about how our ideas would look in reality.

right Sketch models were developed in a variety of materials including wire, acrylic, wood and card: *"In the early days we all wondered what would happen to the shapes we were making. But most of those shapes have actually been realised. It's amazing to have worked with those bits of card and acrylic and then look at the project and see that it's real."* Ben Bisek

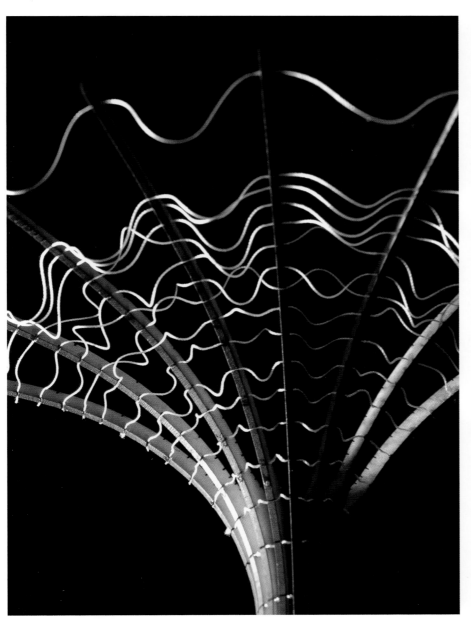

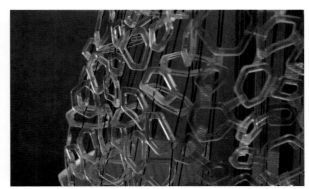

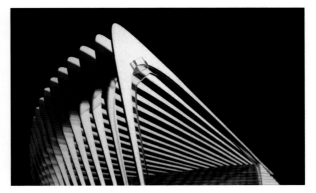

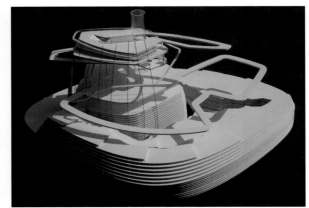

Multi-dimensional thinking

Matthew Potter
Associate Director, Wilkinson Eyre Architects

It may seem tautological to describe the design process of the cooled conservatories as 'multi-dimensional' but from the start of the competition submission until even the last few weeks of snagging, the building was conceived, given form and refined in three dimensions using computer models, physical models—some printed in part from the CAD files—and debates on-site, drawing from and responding to the emerging building itself. The distinction between a 'design' phase and a 'build' phase were therefore blurred.

Whilst this might paint a rather romantic picture of us sculpting the building until we were satisfied with a perfect form, in reality the construction process was driven by a very pragmatic need to find solutions on site by both the designers and the contractors within a short time frame; this was sometimes through negotiation, often collaborative, but rarely in our experience through recourse to the contract.

NParks set a very fast programme for this complex and intricately coordinated building. The actual design phase was significantly compressed after confirmation of the approved budget, and the staggered phasing of different design packages heightened the need for a fast response to optimise levels of coordination.

The design of the project was split into packages and phased in order to allow release of packages of work early, as might normally be expected when working to a tight programme. However, in hindsight, a lot of these programming decisions may have been predicated on what is normally achievable with a more 'standard' building—for example, the air-conditioning and mechanical ventilation systems (ACMV) package for the conservatories was tendered separately and some time after the main contract. Whilst this would be usual practice for a conventional office building—which has easily anticipated cooling loads and in which reasonable ceiling voids can be left for the future routing of designed services that are yet to be designed—it posed more of a challenge for the cooled conservatories which have very particular internal requirements both in terms of their landscape and environmental conditions.

Of course this is by no means 'a standard building'. Achieving the necessary growing conditions represented a major environmental challenge: the exhibited plants require as much daylight as possible, cool air and near constant irrigation; the structure must cast as little shadow as possible, the glass must filter out the heat and misters and foggers are used in the Cloud Forest to load the air with moisture; one building contains a 35-metre high waterfall and the other huge 35-tonne baobabs; there are either planted beds or pedestrian routes over M&E distribution ducts, which also need to be able to take the weight of huge cranes capable of lifting huge trees.

Design programme efficiencies were anticipated because of the use of the standard Singaporean public sector building contract—the Public Sector Standard Conditions of Contract (PSSCOC) – in which the contractor is required to entirely redraw the construction drawings provided by the design team. Essentially the contractor is expected to detail the design provided, which is why design programme efficiencies can normally be found, but is not expected to find solutions to any problems revealed in the design by detailing it. This undoubtedly works well with a 'standard' building type but presents more of a challenge with complicated ones like the cooled conservatories: there were very few standard material

or system applications in the front of house areas and so the vast majority of interfaces needed frequent review, drawing and thinking about in detail.

Whilst the UK team had established a high level of collaboration and focus from the intensity of the design process, moving the project to Singapore and handing over design responsibility inevitably meant a further change in cohesion. Local consultants were presented with the unenviable task of taking over a scheme that was not straightforward and that they would ultimately have to take responsibility for.

previous page Waterfront view of the Cloud Forest under construction

above The scaffolded form of the Cloud Forest takes shape prior to glazing

above The vast scale of the Flower Dome becomes apparent during construction

At times the dogmatic application of building codes, created in part by onerous local professional liability laws, meant that a number of compromises had to be made that might in other situations have been reasoned away: a blanket minimum 2.4-metre headroom everywhere, fire-protection sprinklers above water features and a bizarre allowance for snow load on the façade, which was partially reduced through negotiation but not completely excluded. In addition, the perceived value of achieving a particular generic building 'standard' meant that, for example, any grade of architectural fair-faced concrete was not considered a high-quality finish and therefore ruled out.

The building has a very particular geometry. Its perimeter is different at each and every level, and our desire to create a variable topography within the enclosure as part of the interior landscape design meant that conventional floor plans set at recognisable floor levels were of limited use. ACMV layouts are normally done in rectilinear plant rooms, which are usually the sole preserve of the M&E engineers, or in ceiling voids—which are by and large consistent on each floor—and not under irrigated planter beds which all have variable soil depth and gradient.

100

top left Wilkinson Eyre's Ivy Chan on site at Gardens by the Bay

top right Inside the Cloud Forest mountain during construction

bottom The Flower Dome with steel ribs in situ

The challenges associated with the unique geometry were compounded by the limited use of 3D CAD models within the wider team. The project started in the days before the widespread advent of building information modelling (BIM) which sees the building modelled digitally in three dimensions from the earliest stages of design with consultants from different disciplines contributing to a central model. The local consultant team we worked with did not at that time make use of 3D CAD models and were very wary of issuing our 3D information—amongst the design team itself and, in particular, to the contractor. By contrast the contractor was desperate to be issued the model so as to simply better understand the space and the construction complexity. In the end 3D data was issued to the contractor 'for information only'.

To build this project in the way that we did relied on the extremely collaborative, positive influence of the main contractor. Woh Hup are Singaporean and proud of both their ability and their part in creating this major landmark building at the entrance to Singapore. Their team was led by a great contracts manager, Mr Guna Gunasekaran, who—at times almost cartoonish in his demonstrations of rage or delight during meetings about the building and its design—drove the build process with relentless enthusiasm and commitment.

The requirement for all architecture in Singapore to be delivered by a 'qualified person' (QP) meant that Wilkinson Eyre was expected to take more of a back-seat role in the build-phase of the project. However, the complexity of the building and the ongoing issues generated by the design process described above meant that Wilkinson Eyre retained a presence of never less than two full-time staff in Singapore until the day the building opened. Many of the design team moved to Singapore from London on a semi-permanent basis— Gabi Code for four years, Bosco Lam and Ivy Chan for two and a half –with others, myself included, arriving for long stays during critical periods. We have vivid memories of our time in the city: delicious chicken rice, standing (and rarely walking) on escalators, and trying to speak convincing Sing-lish.

The 'build' phase was therefore interlaced with 'design' and characterised by enormous and at times unwieldy technical meetings of four or five hours long. In Singapore, rooms will often have a meeting table and then one or two perimeter rows of seats for what might only be described as observers or bit-part players who will contribute when directly addressed by those at the table but will otherwise spend their time furiously texting or, in calmer moments, dozing off. The contractor bought the room lunch on more than one occasion in order to keep everyone at the table and the Woh Hup architectural team (a squad of fierce but hugely experienced women) brought biscuits in their handbags which they would nibble furtively when lunch wasn't provided. This prompted under the radar discussions with the contractor and role-playing where we would pretend in official 'contractual' meetings that earlier discussions had not already taken place. Gaining the trust of the contractor was of paramount importance and by demonstrating our value to them without skating too close to the contractual edge we were able to expedite the process. This was certainly recognised but never formally condoned by the contract administrator.

Gabi remembers there was also a certain pecking order on the site—not only did we have to gain the contractors' trust, we also had to gain their professional respect. We were told by local colleagues that consultants didn't need to wear high-visibility vests on site: "Only the workers wear high-viz vests, and you don't want to look like a worker". Most of the workers on site were Bangladeshi or Indian, and had come to Singapore to find work. Many were living in cramped dormitories, leaving their wives and children behind at home for years at a time. They often worked in very challenging conditions—at the top of the Cloud Forest it could get up to 50°C before the cooling systems were in place, and workers could be at height for hours at a time. During the lunchtime hours, hundreds of the workers would retreat to the huge, cool plant rooms beneath the buildings to rest—and this became a favourite time for the UK team to walk around the eerily quiet site.

To help counter this, the client worked hard to create a collective spirit. For example, work to install the baobabs in the Flower Dome began at 5pm one afternoon when all other construction finished for the day. Contractors, horticulturalists, client representatives and consultants were all left on site. It took hours to do, and in the early hours of the morning Dr Tan went out and bought every single person there burgers and fries. They only finished installing the baobab at around midday the following day.

Local construction methods and the tight programme meant that there was a need for continual site presence to ensure things were not built before they were designed or fully understood to avoid the need for them to be ordered or negotiated down. There was a lot of site discussion over partially completed work and we became adept at developing quick 3D CAD models in Rhino, sketching over them or photographs from site and packaging them in Powerpoint slideshows to demonstrate sequential design derivation, negotiate amendments or illustrate construction build-up. Hand sketches and mark-ups

left Workers take a midday rest in the cool interior of the Cloud Forest

right The largest of the bottle trees arrives at the Flower Dome

over prints of Rhino models or photographs of the building were also used to convey our design intent. We were often challenging local working practices. After one early meeting a young contractor came up and said "Are all buildings in the UK curvy? You know, straight buildings are much easier to build."

We submitted our expression of interest (EOI) for the competition on 28 February 2006, were shortlisted on 5 April, announced as winners of the competition on 17 August, and held our first design workshop with NParks in Singapore at the beginning of October. We worked on refining the masterplan until March 2007, began work on the conservatories at the end of June, and value-engineered the project in line with the confirmed

budget in October of the same year. The project broke ground in November, with Dr Tan and the other VIPs wielding their golden shovels in front of the press, and submitted the Stage C report for the entire building in September 2008. The façade contract was awarded at the end of the same month, the main contract in February 2009, and we showcased the completed Flower Dome for the World Orchid Conference on 11 November 2011. Both cooled conservatories—along with the rest of the Bay South gardens—opened on 29 June 2012.

It was a real pleasure to attend the opening and see people enjoying the building and doing all the things we hoped they would do. I think even after six years on

   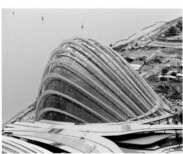

above Sequences showing the conservatories during construction

the project, most of us on the team still walk through the main entrance into the Flower Dome and think "Wow"! It is a project with real purpose, occasionally contentious, but ultimately—we hope—a great success. At the time of writing this it is creeping up the rankings on Trip Advisor. The reviews make for compelling reading and trigger very fond memories of the whole process. Winning the World Architecture Festival (WAF) Building of the Year Award in 2012 was a great way to complete our design journey: a fitting testament to an extraordinary project, commissioned by a very clear-sighted client and requiring extraordinary levels of collaboration, commitment and endurance from the whole team.

Plants and people

Paul Baker

We knew right from the beginning that Gardens by the Bay would be a once-in-a-lifetime project. At its heart was an extraordinarily tough brief: whereas elsewhere in the world glasshouses are normally used to produce a warm growing environment, the conservatories at Bay South had to create cool conditions within the context of Singapore's humid tropical climate—and in as sustainable a way as possible.

Wilkinson Eyre's approach has always promoted the idea of cross-disciplinary collaboration between technical and artistic disciplines, but we have never before worked on a project that demanded from the outset such a thorough integration of skills. It is this collaboration—the fact that the project was a team effort in every way—that has ultimately delivered an incredible building. In putting together the team, Andrew Grant chose collaborators who not only had personal experience of working together, and enjoyed doing it, but whose design philosophy combined a commitment to the environment with an instinctive understanding of placemaking. And so the project is not just about one genius idea, realised by others, but is instead about this team working closely together to solve problems and collectively make a beautiful, appropriate and original architecture. The architecture and structural design of the conservatories is deeply influenced by the horticultural narrative and the environmental strategy—and vice versa.

Even at the competition stage, we began to appreciate the incredible foresightedness and intelligence of our clients at NParks—and the scale of their ambition for the new garden. Particular credit and respect should go to Dr Tan, Kenneth Er, Andy Kwek, Ng Boon Gee and Anton van der Schans, who supported us throughout the entire project. They were willing to embrace creative, innovative ideas, and were not afraid to pursue their initial vision that this should be one of the world's great tropical gardens, "designed to standards of creativity that are comparable to the best in the world".

Potentially, Gardens by the Bay will be experienced by millions of overseas visitors, but at the same time they create a new, green 'living room' for the city's residents, embodying Singapore's vision for "A City in a Garden" and providing a place for recreation and celebration. One of the great joys of this project has been seeing people experience the gardens at first hand, and watching their reactions as they marvel at the scale of the Flower Dome and shiver at the surprising coolness and wetness of the Cloud Forest, children flinging their arms wide in delight at the drama of the waterfall. People are now populating the conservatories in their own way—celebrating weddings and family get-togethers, playing with the kids and meeting friends, enjoying a break from the heat outside or simply taking hundreds of photographs. These spontaneous responses are extremely gratifying, and are confirmation of the conservatories' ability to move and excite people.

Team credits

Architect: Wilkinson Eyre Architects

Lead design for cooled conservatories, associated infrastructure and central visitor hub; design of rooftop bar and vertical access for 50m supertree; concept design for principal buildings within Bay South Garden

Main team

Paul Baker (project director), Ivy Chan, Gary Chapman, Joseph Chisholm, Yuni Choi, Charlie Coates, Gabi Code, Ben Dawson, Lisa Dew, Jim Eyre, Helen Floate, Julia Glynn Smith, Joerg Hansen, Elizabeth Hughes, Alex Kyriakides, Dan Ladyman, Adrian Lai, Bosco Lam, Jeff Lee, Kirk MacDonnell, Vinny Patel, Tuomas Pirinen, Matthew Potter (project architect), Oscar Rodriguez, Owen Rutter, Jonathan Shaw, Mark Summerfield, Chris Wilkinson, Lesta Woo, Soo Yau (project secretary), Jing Zhi Kee

Also involved

Ben Bisek, Eleanor Boardman, Tia Chim, Eleanor Dodman, Thomas Dunn, Daniel Gebreiter, Damian Groves, Ben Hartwell, Min Li, Leszek Marszalek, Catherine Moyes, Massimo Napoleoni, Eleni Pavlidou, Thomas Rigby, Ville Saarikoski, Tom Smith, Ivan Subanovic, Neil Taylor

Media

Emma Keyte, Michelle Lewis, Margit Millstein, Rita Patel, Damon Richardson

Admin (London)

Daniela Fogosova, Courtenay Holden, Kim Towers, Naomi Vaughan, Fiona Wheelwright, Bethany Wren

Admin (Singapore)

Tricia Auyong, Iris Chan, Amy Mak

Masterplanner/landscape architect: Grant Associates

Assembly of core design team; overall masterplan for Bay South Garden, project co-ordination, detail design and implementation; design of cooled conservatories internal landscape; design of supertrees including aerial walkway; design of themed gardens and horticultural structures

Environmental engineer: Atelier Ten

Environmental design consultancy; building services engineering; daylight analysis; energy and thermal modelling; central energy infrastructure

Structural engineer: Atelier One

Structural engineering design for supertrees, aerial walkway, cooled conservatory enclosures, other structures throughout site

Horticulturalist (and client): NParks (now Gardens by the Bay)

Intepretation consultant: Land Design Studio

Cost consultant: Langdon & Seah Singapore Pte

Engineering support: Meinhardt (Infastructure) Pte

Architecture/engineering support: CPG Corporation

Project management: PM Link Pte

Design management: Buro Four

Lighting design: Spiers & Major / Lighting Planners Associates

Acoustics: Arup / VPAC

Fire engineering: Arup

Façade engineering: Arup

Communication designer: Thomas Matthews

Filmmaker/animator: Squint Opera

Irrigation design: WET (Water Equipment Technology)

Main contractor: Woh Hup Pte Ltd

Facts and figures

Gardens at Bay South

Project value: £350 million
Gross area of garden: 54 hectares
Gross area of conservatory complex: 24,500sqm

Cool dry conservatory (Flower Dome)

Dimensions to superstructure: 183m x 130m x 38m
Dimensions to glass envelope: 170m x 86m x 35m
Gross area: 12,790sqm
Area under glass: 10,100sqm
Planted displays: 4,570sqm (of which 848sqm is the Flower Field)
Volume: 195,000 cubic metres
Façade surface area: 16,000sqm comprising 3,332 panels of 42 main sizes
Largest glazing panel: 3m x 2m
Smallest glazing panel: 0.82m x 2.88m
External shading: 196 shades
Largest shade: 44sqm
Smallest shade: 24.5sqm
Capacity: 1,400 pax
Event space capacity: 1,000 pax
Climate: Mediterranean
Temperature: 23-25°C (day), 17°C (night), 13°C (ignition)
Relative humidity: 60% (day), 80% (night), 80% (ignition)
Light levels: 45,000lux for more than 5.4% of annual daylit hours

Cool moist conservatory (Cloud Forest)

Dimensions to superstructure: 123m x 95m x 58m
Dimensions to glass envelope: 118m x 77m x 54m
Gross area: 7,310sqm
Area under glass: 6,300sqm
Planted displays: 2,145sqm (with additional 3,800sqm vertical planting)
Volume: 153,000 cubic metres
Façade surface area: 12,600sqm comprising 2,577 panels of 690 main sizes
Largest glazing panel: 3m x 2m
Smallest glazing panel: 1.86m x 2.88m
External shading: 223 shades
Largest shade: 47sqm
Smallest shade: 16sqm
Height of mountain: 40m
Height of waterfall: 35m
Capacity: 1,200 pax
Climate: Tropical montane
Temperature: 23-25°C (day), 17°C (night), 16°C (ignition)
Relative humidity: 80%+ (day), 80%+ (night), 80%+ (ignition)
Light levels: 45,000lux for more than 5.4% of annual daylit hours

Structure

Composite structure comprising steel gridshell supported by a superstructure of radially arranged steel ribs
Flower Dome
Arches (inc. struts and ties) 1,153 tons (= 0.59 tons per linear metre)
Gridshell (inc. bracing) 717 tons
Total 1,870 tons (= 0.11 tons per sqm of structure)
Cloud Forest
Arches (inc. struts and ties) 790 tons (= 0.59 tons per linear metre)
Gridshell (inc. bracing) 504 tons
Total 1,294 tons (= 0.10 tons per sqm of structure)

Envelope

Low-e coated glazing with automated retractable fabric shades
Flower Dome
Façade surface area: 16,000sqm comprising 3,332 panels of 42 main sizes
Largest glazing panel: 3m x 2m
Smallest glazing panel: 0.82m x 2.88m
External shading: 196 shades
Largest shade: 44sqm
Smallest shade: 24.5sqm
Cloud Forest
Façade surface area: 12,600sqm comprising 2,577 panels of 690 main sizes
Largest glazing panel: 3m x 2m
Smallest glazing panel: 1.86m x 2.88m
External shading: 223 shades
Largest shade: 47sqm
Smallest shade: 16sqm

Timeline

Expression of interest: February/March 2006

Shortlisted for competition: April 2006

Competition period: May—August 2006

Presentation interviews: September 2006

Competition winner announced: September 2006

Masterplan completed: February 2007

Stage C complete: September 2007

Groundbreaking: November 2007

Stage D complete: January 2008

Main construction period: January 2008—November 2011

Soft opening: November 2011

Completion: June 2012

Contributor biographies

Dr Tan Wee Kiat is the visionary behind Gardens by the Bay—and our client for the project. He retired as CEO of NParks in 2006, when he was appointed advisor to NParks and Project Director of Gardens by the Bay. As a leading horticulturalist, he led the selection and sourcing of plants throughout.

Nigel Taylor is Director of the Singapore Botanic Gardens and was Curator of Horticulture at the Royal Botanic Gardens, Kew from 1995 to 2011.

Jim Eyre is a Director of Wilkinson Eyre Architects. He worked on the concept for Gardens by the Bay, and the refinement of the geometry, form, detailing and shading of the glasshouse envelopes. He was awarded an OBE for his services to architecture in 2003.

Paul Baker is a Director of Wilkinson Eyre Architects and led the Gardens by the Bay design team, spending extended periods in Singapore throughout the project. He has a particular interest in holistic design and buildings which reinforce an experiential narrative for users.

Matthew Potter is an Associate Director of Wilkinson Eyre Architects and was project architect for the cool conservatories, leading the practice's Singapore office throughout the construction period.

Andrew Grant is founder of Grant Associates, and with his team led the overall masterplan for Gardens by the Bay. In 2012 he was made a Royal Designer for Industry (RDI) in recognition of his pioneering work in landscape architecture.

Patrick Bellew is founder of environmental engineers Atelier Ten and has a unique reputation for integrating innovative technologies with high-profile architecture, for which he was made an Honorary Fellow of the RIBA in 2001.

Neil Thomas is director and founder of Atelier One, a highly innovative engineering practice which researches and develops structural solutions on a variety of scales.

Peter Higgins is creative director of Land Design Studio, a cross-disciplinary design practice specialising in exhibition design and interpretation.

Emma Keyte is former Head of Communications at Wilkinson Eyre Architects and worked on the original competition for Gardens by the Bay in 2006. She is now a freelance consultant to the practice, and acted as editor, project manager and writer of the design sections for *Supernature*.

Image credits

Atelier One: 45 (bottom right)

Atelier Ten: 64, 65

Grant Associates: 40 (bottom right), 42, 43 (right), 68, 70, 71, 88 (bottom left and right)

Nick Guttridge: 13 (top right)

NParks: 40 (3 diagrams bottom left)

Andrew Putler: 40 (top)

Craig Sheppard: front cover, 6, 14, 17, 18, 20, 22, 23, 24, 25, 26-27, 28, 44 (bottom), 46 (top), 51 (top), 54, 57, 61, 72, 74 (bottom left), 76, 79 (top, bottom left, bottom right), 80, 81, 87 (top right), 96, 100 (bottom), 103, 104-105, 112, inside back cover

Darren Soh: 2, 8, 21, 52, 59 (top centre), 74 (top), 98, 99

Squint Opera: 39

Robert Such: 4, 67, 83 (right), 85

Max Tan: inside front cover

Corbis Images: 43 (left)

Getty Images: 111 (top right)

Mary Evans/Grenville Collins Postcard Collection: 10 (top left and bottom)

Mary Evans/Grosvenor Prints: 12 (bottom)

Mary Evans/Illustrated London News: 12 (top)

Mary Evans Picture Library: 12 (middle)

Nature Picture Library/Pete Oxford: 77 (middle)

Nature Picture Library/Visuals Unlimited: 77 (top)

RIBA Library Photographs Collection: 10 (top right), 62 (left)

RIBA Library Photographs Collection/Eric de Maré: 62 (right)

Sketches on pages 36-37 with thanks to our co-consultants

All other images, drawings and visualisations: Wilkinson Eyre Architects

Special thanks

Paul Baker

Many people have contributed to the success of Gardens by the Bay: architects, landscapers, engineers, contractors, administrators and advisors; the NParks client and horticultural teams; and indeed the many people who have visited in the last few months.

In helping to produce this book we are especially grateful to Dr Tan Wee Kiat, Nigel Taylor, Edwin Heathcote, Patrick Bellew, Neil Thomas, Peter Higgins, Jim Eyre and Matthew Potter for their contributions, invaluable insights and continuing collaboration, enthusiasm and unwavering support, indicative of the spirit adopted from the outset. Thanks also to Gordon Goff and his team at ORO for taking us on and to Craig Sheppard, Darren Soh and Robert Such for some excellent photographs.

None of this would have been possible without Wilkinson Eyre's team, so I thank them for their hard work and generosity with their time. We are particularly grateful to Ivy Chan, Gabi Code, Adrian Lai and Bosco Lam for their incredible work on site in Singapore and to Alex Kyriakides for his help in developing the building envelope.

I must expressly thank Emma Keyte for helping us tell our exciting story, ensuring our words do our architecture justice and providing patient encouragement along the way. We also thank Margit Millstein for her skillful eye and beautiful composition, and Andrés de Santiago Areizaga for completing the design.

We are grateful for Dr Tan and his team's vision, and their drive to realise such an ambitious project. My particular thanks go to Andy Kwek who balanced the budgets and endured the many phone calls from me during the last six years with good humour and great patience.

Finally, my biggest thanks go to Andrew Grant, for thinking of us, picking up the phone and asking us to join the fun.